Ethics

Collected Readings

Ethics

Collected Readings

Jean W. Rioux
Benedictine College

Wipf & Stock
PUBLISHERS
Eugene, Oregon

Wipf and Stock Publishers
199 W. 8th Avenue
Eugene, Oregon 97401
Www.wipfandstock.com

Ethics: Collected Readings
By Jean W. Rioux
Copyright © 2005 by Jean W. Rioux
ISBN: 1-59752-290-2

Contents

Acknowledgments

Plato's *Euthyphro*, translated by Jowett, 1871.

Epicurus' *Letter to Menoeceus*, translated by Hicks, 1925.

Epictetus' *Enchiridion*, translated by Carter, 1758.

Augustine of Hippo, *City of God*, translated by Dods, 1876.

Boethius, *Consolation of Philosophy*, translated by Cooper, 1902.

Thomas Aquinas, *Treatise on Law*, in *Summa Theologica*, translated by Fathers of the English Dominican Province, 1947.

Immanuel Kant, *Fundamental Principles of the Metaphysics of Morals*, translated by Abbott, 1889.

Plato, *Euthyphro*

Euthyphro. Why have you left the Lyceum, Socrates? and what are you doing in the Porch of the King Archon? Surely you cannot be concerned in a suit before the King, like myself?

Socrates. Not in a suit, Euthyphro; impeachment is the word which the Athenians use.

Euth. What! I suppose that some one has been prosecuting you, for I cannot believe that you are the prosecutor of another.

Soc. Certainly not.

Euth. Then some one else has been prosecuting you?

Soc. Yes.

Euth. And who is he?

Soc. A young man who is little known, Euthyphro; and I hardly know him: his name is Meletus, and he is of the deme of Pitthis. Perhaps you may remember his appearance; he has a beak, and long straight hair, and a beard which is ill grown.

Euth. No, I do not remember him, Socrates. But what is the charge which he brings against you?

Soc. What is the charge? Well, a very serious charge, which shows a good deal of character in the young man, and for which he is certainly not to be despised. He says he knows how the youth are corrupted and who are their corruptors. I fancy that he must be a wise man, and seeing that I am the reverse of a wise man, he has found me out, and is going to accuse me of corrupting his young friends. And of this our mother the state is to be the judge. Of all our political men he is the only one who seems to me to begin in the right way, with the cultivation of virtue in youth; like a good husbandman, he makes the young shoots his first care, and clears away us who are the destroyers of them. This is only the first step; he will afterwards attend to the elder branches; and if he goes on as he has begun, he will be a very great public benefactor.

Euth. I hope that he may; but I rather fear, Socrates, that the opposite will turn out to be the truth. My opinion is that in attacking you he is simply aiming a blow at the foundation of the state. But in what way does he say that you corrupt the young?

Soc. He brings a wonderful accusation against me, which at first hearing excites surprise: he says that I am a poet or maker of gods,

1

and that I invent new gods and deny the existence of old ones; this is the ground of his indictment.

Euth. I understand, Socrates; he means to attack you about the familiar sign which occasionally, as you say, comes to you. He thinks that you are a neologian, and he is going to have you up before the court for this. He knows that such a charge is readily received by the world, as I myself know too well; for when I speak in the assembly about divine things, and foretell the future to them, they laugh at me and think me a madman. Yet every word that I say is true. But they are jealous of us all; and we must be brave and go at them.

Soc. Their laughter, friend Euthyphro, is not a matter of much consequence. For a man may be thought wise; but the Athenians, I suspect, do not much trouble themselves about him until he begins to impart his wisdom to others, and then for some reason or other, perhaps, as you say, from jealousy, they are angry.

Euth. I am never likely to try their temper in this way.

Soc. I dare say not, for you are reserved in your behavior, and seldom impart your wisdom. But I have a benevolent habit of pouring out myself to everybody, and would even pay for a listener, and I am afraid that the Athenians may think me too talkative. Now if, as I was saying, they would only laugh at me, as you say that they laugh at you, the time might pass gaily enough in the court; but perhaps they may be in earnest, and then what the end will be you soothsayers only can predict.

Euth. I dare say that the affair will end in nothing, Socrates, and that you will win your cause; and I think that I shall win my own.

Soc. And what is your suit, Euthyphro? are you the pursuer or the defendant?

Euth. I am the pursuer.

Soc. Of whom?

Euth. You will think me mad when I tell you.

Soc. Why, has the fugitive wings?

Euth. Nay, he is not very volatile at his time of life.

Soc. Who is he?

Euth. My father.

Soc. Your father! my good man?

Euth. Yes.

75 **Soc.** And of what is he accused?

Euth. Of murder, Socrates.

Soc. By the powers, Euthyphro! how little does the common herd know of the nature of right and truth. A man must be an extraordinary man, and have made great strides in wisdom, before
80 he could have seen his way to bring such an action.

Euth. Indeed, Socrates, he must.

Soc. I suppose that the man whom your father murdered was one of your relatives—clearly he was; for if he had been a stranger you would never have thought of prosecuting him.

85 **Euth.** I am amused, Socrates, at your making a distinction between one who is a relation and one who is not a relation; for surely the pollution is the same in either case, if you knowingly associate with the murderer when you ought to clear yourself and him by proceeding against him. The real question is whether the
90 murdered man has been justly slain. If justly, then your duty is to let the matter alone; but if unjustly, then even if the murderer lives under the same roof with you and eats at the same table, proceed against him. Now the man who is dead was a poor dependent of mine who worked for us as a field laborer on our farm in Naxos, and
95 one day in a fit of drunken passion he got into a quarrel with one of our domestic servants and slew him. My father bound him hand and foot and threw him into a ditch, and then sent to Athens to ask of a diviner what he should do with him. Meanwhile he never attended to him and took no care about him, for he regarded him as a murderer;
100 and thought that no great harm would be done even if he did die. Now this was just what happened. For such was the effect of cold and hunger and chains upon him, that before the messenger returned from the diviner, he was dead. And my father and family are angry with me for taking the part of the murderer and prosecuting my
105 father. They say that he did not kill him, and that if he did, dead man was but a murderer, and I ought not to take any notice, for that a son is impious who prosecutes a father. Which shows, Socrates, how little they know what the gods think about piety and impiety.

Soc. Good heavens, Euthyphro! and is your knowledge of religion
110 and of things pious and impious so very exact, that, supposing the circumstances to be as you state them, you are not afraid lest you too

may be doing an impious thing in bringing an action against your father?

Euth. The best of Euthyphro, and that which distinguishes him, Socrates, from other men, is his exact knowledge of all such matters. What should I be good for without it?

Soc. Rare friend! I think that I cannot do better than be your disciple. Then before the trial with Meletus comes on I shall challenge him, and say that I have always had a great interest in religious questions, and now, as he charges me with rash imaginations and innovations in religion, I have become your disciple. You, Meletus, as I shall say to him, acknowledge Euthyphro to be a great theologian, and sound in his opinions; and if you approve of him you ought to approve of me, and not have me into court; but if you disapprove, you should begin by indicting him who is my teacher, and who will be the ruin, not of the young, but of the old; that is to say, of myself whom he instructs, and of his old father whom he admonishes and chastises. And if Meletus refuses to listen to me, but will go on, and will not shift the indictment from me to you, I cannot do better than repeat this challenge in the court.

Euth. Yes, indeed, Socrates; and if he attempts to indict me I am mistaken if I do not find a flaw in him; the court shall have a great deal more to say to him than to me.

Soc. And I, my dear friend, knowing this, am desirous of becoming your disciple. For I observe that no one appears to notice you— not even this Meletus; but his sharp eyes have found me out at once, and he has indicted me for impiety. And therefore, I adjure you to tell me the nature of piety and impiety, which you said that you knew so well, and of murder, and of other offences against the gods. What are they? Is not piety in every action always the same? and impiety, again— is it not always the opposite of piety, and also the same with itself, having, as impiety, one notion which includes whatever is impious?

Euth. To be sure, Socrates.

Soc. And what is piety, and what is impiety?

Euth. Piety is doing as I am doing; that is to say, prosecuting any one who is guilty of murder, sacrilege, or of any similar crime—whether he be your father or mother, or whoever he may be—that makes no difference; and not to prosecute them is impiety.

150 And please to consider, Socrates, what a notable proof I will give you
of the truth of my words, a proof which I have already given to
others:—of the principle, I mean, that the impious, whoever he may
be, ought not to go unpunished. For do not men regard Zeus as the
best and most righteous of the gods?—and yet they admit that he

155 bound his father (Cronos) because he wickedly devoured his sons,
and that he too had punished his own father (Uranus) for a similar
reason, in a nameless manner. And yet when I proceed against my
father, they are angry with me. So inconsistent are they in their way
of talking when the gods are concerned, and when I am concerned.

160 **Soc.** May not this be the reason, Euthyphro, why I am charged
with impiety—that I cannot away with these stories about the gods?
and therefore I suppose that people think me wrong. But, as you who
are well informed about them approve of them, I cannot do better
than assent to your superior wisdom. What else can I say, confessing

165 as I do, that I know nothing about them? Tell me, for the love of
Zeus, whether you really believe that they are true.

Euth. Yes, Socrates; and things more wonderful still, of which
the world is in ignorance.

Soc. And do you really believe that the gods, fought with one

170 another, and had dire quarrels, battles, and the like, as the poets
say, and as you may see represented in the works of great artists?
The temples are full of them; and notably the robe of Athena, which
is carried up to the Acropolis at the great Panathenaea, is
embroidered with them. Are all these tales of the gods true,

175 Euthyphro?

Euth. Yes, Socrates; and, as I was saying, I can tell you, if you
would like to hear them, many other things about the gods which
would quite amaze you.

Soc. I dare say; and you shall tell me them at some other time

180 when I have leisure. But just at present I would rather hear from you
a more precise answer, which you have not as yet given, my friend, to
the question, What is "piety"? When asked, you only replied, Doing
as you do, charging your father with murder.

Euth. And what I said was true, Socrates.

185 **Soc.** No doubt, Euthyphro; but you would admit that there are
many other pious acts?

Euth. There are.

Soc. Remember that I did not ask you to give me two or three examples of piety, but to explain the general idea which makes all pious things to be pious. Do you not recollect that there was one idea which made the impious, impious, and the pious, pious?

Euth. I remember.

Soc. Tell me what is the nature of this idea, and then I shall have a standard to which I may look, and by which I may measure actions, whether yours or those of any one else, and then I shall be able to say that such and such an action is pious, such another impious.

Euth. I will tell you, if you like.

Soc. I should very much like.

Euth. Piety, then, is that which is dear to the gods, and impiety is that which is not dear to them.

Soc. Very good, Euthyphro; you have now given me the sort of answer which I wanted. But whether what you say is true or not I cannot as yet tell, although I make no doubt that you will prove the truth of your words.

Euth. Of course.

Soc. Come, then, and let us examine what we are saying. That thing or person which is dear to the gods is pious, and that thing or person which is hateful to the gods is impious, these two being the extreme opposites of one another. Was not that said?

Euth. It was.

Soc. And well said?

Euth. Yes, Socrates, I thought so; it was certainly said.

Soc. And further, Euthyphro, the gods were admitted to have enmities and hatreds and differences?

Euth. Yes, that was also said.

Soc. And what sort of difference creates enmity and anger? Suppose for example that you and I, my good friend, differ about a number; do differences of this sort make us enemies and set us at variance with one another? Do we not go at once to arithmetic, and put an end to them by a sum?

Euth. True.

Soc. Or suppose that we differ about magnitudes, do we not quickly end the differences by measuring?

Euth. Very true.

Soc. And we end a controversy about heavy and light by resorting to a weighing machine?

Euth. To be sure.

230 **Soc.** But what differences are there which cannot be thus decided, and which therefore make us angry and set us at enmity with one another? I dare say the answer does not occur to you at the moment, and therefore I will suggest that these enmities arise when the matters of difference are the just and unjust, good and evil, honorable and dishonorable. Are not these the points about which 235 men differ, and about which when we are unable satisfactorily to decide our differences, you and I and all of us quarrel, when we do quarrel?

Euth. Yes, Socrates, the nature of the differences about which we quarrel is such as you describe.

240 **Soc.** And the quarrels of the gods, noble Euthyphro, when they occur, are of a like nature?

Euth. Certainly they are.

Soc. They have differences of opinion, as you say, about good and evil, just and unjust, honorable and dishonorable: there would have 245 been no quarrels among them, if there had been no such differences—would there now?

Euth. You are quite right.

Soc. Does not every man love that which he deems noble and just and good, and hate the opposite of them?

250 **Euth.** Very true.

Soc. But, as you say, people regard the same things, some as just and others as unjust,—about these they dispute; and so there arise wars and fighting among them.

Euth. Very true.

255 **Soc.** Then the same things are hated by the gods and loved by the gods, and are both hateful and dear to them?

Euth. True.

Soc. And upon this view the same things, Euthyphro, will be pious and also impious?

260 **Euth.** So I should suppose.

Soc. Then, my friend, I remark with surprise that you have not answered the question which I asked. For I certainly did not ask you to tell me what action is both pious and impious: but now it would

seem that what is loved by the gods is also hated by them. And
therefore, Euthyphro, in thus chastising your father you may very
likely be doing what is agreeable to Zeus but disagreeable to Cronos
or Uranus, and what is acceptable to Hephaestus but unacceptable
to Here, and there may be other gods who have similar differences of
opinion.

Euth. But I believe, Socrates, that all the gods would be agreed
as to the propriety of punishing a murderer: there would be no
difference of opinion about that.

Soc. Well, but speaking of men, Euthyphro, did you ever hear
any one arguing that a murderer or any sort of evil-doer ought to be
let off?

Euth. I should rather say that these are the questions which
they are always arguing, especially in courts of law: they commit all
sorts of crimes, and there is nothing which they will not do or say in
their own defense.

Soc. But do they admit their guilt, Euthyphro, and yet say that
they ought not to be punished?

Euth. No; they do not.

Soc. Then there are some things which they do not venture to
say and do: for they do not venture to argue that the guilty are to be
unpunished, but they deny their guilt, do they not?

Euth. Yes.

Soc. Then they do not argue that the evil-doer should not be
punished, but they argue about the fact of who the evil-doer is, and
what he did and when?

Euth. True.

Soc. And the gods are in the same case, if as you assert they
quarrel about just and unjust, and some of them say while others
deny that injustice is done among them. For surely neither God nor
man will ever venture to say that the doer of injustice is not to be
punished?

Euth. That is true, Socrates, in the main.

Soc. But they join issue about the particulars—gods and men
alike; and, if they dispute at all, they dispute about some act which
is called in question, and which by some is affirmed to be just, by
others to be unjust. Is not that true?

Euth. Quite true.

Soc. Well then, my dear friend Euthyphro, do tell me, for my better instruction and information, what proof have you that in the opinion of all the gods a servant who is guilty of murder, and is put in chains by the master of the dead man, and dies because he is put in chains before he who bound him can learn from the interpreters of the gods what he ought to do with him, dies unjustly; and that on behalf of such an one a son ought to proceed against his father and accuse him of murder. How would you show that all the gods absolutely agree in approving of his act? Prove to me that they do, and I will applaud your wisdom as long as I live.

Euth. It will be a difficult task; but I could make the matter very dear indeed to you.

Soc. I understand; you mean to say that I am not so quick of apprehension as the judges: for to them you will be sure to prove that the act is unjust, and hateful to the gods.

Euth. Yes indeed, Socrates; at least if they will listen to me.

Soc. But they will be sure to listen if they find that you are a good speaker. There was a notion that came into my mind while you were speaking; I said to myself: "Well, and what if Euthyphro does prove to me that all the gods regarded the death of the serf as unjust, how do I know anything more of the nature of piety and impiety? for granting that this action may be hateful to the gods, still piety and impiety are not adequately defined by these distinctions, for that which is hateful to the gods has been shown to be also pleasing and dear to them." And therefore, Euthyphro, I do not ask you to prove this; I will suppose, if you like, that all the gods condemn and abominate such an action. But I will amend the definition so far as to say that what all the gods hate is impious, and what they love pious or holy; and what some of them love and others hate is both or neither. Shall this be our definition of piety and impiety?

Euth. Why not, Socrates?

Soc. Why not! certainly, as far as I am concerned, Euthyphro, there is no reason why not. But whether this admission will greatly assist you in the task of instructing me as you promised, is a matter for you to consider.

Euth. Yes, I should say that what all the gods love is pious and holy, and the opposite which they all hate, impious.

340 **Soc.** Ought we to inquire into the truth of this, Euthyphro, or simply to accept the mere statement on our own authority and that of others? What do you say?

Euth. We should inquire; and I believe that the statement will stand the test of enquiry.

345 **Soc.** We shall know better, my good friend, in a little while. The point which I should first wish to understand is whether the pious or holy is beloved by the gods because it is holy, or holy because it is beloved of the gods.

Euth. I do not understand your meaning, Socrates.

350 **Soc.** I will endeavor to explain: we, speak of carrying and we speak of being carried, of leading and being led, seeing and being seen. You know that in all such cases there is a difference, and you know also in what the difference lies?

Euth. I think that I understand.

355 **Soc.** And is not that which is beloved distinct from that which loves?

Euth. Certainly.

Soc. Well; and now tell me, is that which is carried in this state of carrying because it is carried, or for some other reason?

360 **Euth.** No; that is the reason.

Soc. And the same is true of what is led and of what is seen?

Euth. True.

Soc. And a thing is not seen because it is visible, but conversely, visible because it is seen; nor is a thing led because it is in the state

365 of being led, or carried because it is in the state of being carried, but the converse of this. And now I think, Euthyphro, that my meaning will be intelligible; and my meaning is, that any state of action or passion implies previous action or passion. It does not become because it is becoming, but it is in a state of becoming because it

370 becomes; neither does it suffer because it is in a state of suffering, but it is in a state of suffering because it suffers. Do you not agree?

Euth. Yes.

Soc. Is not that which is loved in some state either of becoming or suffering?

375 **Euth.** Yes.

Soc. And the same holds as in the previous instances; the state of being loved follows the act of being loved, and not the act the state.

Euth. Certainly.

Soc. And what do you say of piety, Euthyphro: is not piety, according to your definition, loved by all the gods?

Euth. Yes.

Soc. Because it is pious or holy, or for some other reason?

Euth. No, that is the reason.

Soc. It is loved because it is holy, not holy because it is loved?

Euth. Yes.

Soc. And that which is dear to the gods is loved by them, and is in a state to be loved of them because it is loved of them?

Euth. Certainly.

Soc. Then that which is dear to the gods, Euthyphro, is not holy, nor is that which is holy loved of God, as you affirm; but they are two different things.

Euth. How do you mean, Socrates?

Soc. I mean to say that the holy has been acknowledge by us to be loved of God because it is holy, not to be holy because it is loved.

Euth. Yes.

Soc. But that which is dear to the gods is dear to them because it is loved by them, not loved by them because it is dear to them.

Euth. True.

Soc. But, friend Euthyphro, if that which is holy is the same with that which is dear to God, and is loved because it is holy, then that which is dear to God would have been loved as being dear to God; but if that which dear to God is dear to him because loved by him, then that which is holy would have been holy because loved by him. But now you see that the reverse is the case, and that they are quite different from one another. For one (theophiles) is of a kind to be loved cause it is loved, and the other (osion) is loved because it is of a kind to be loved. Thus you appear to me, Euthyphro, when I ask you what is the essence of holiness, to offer an attribute only, and not the essence—the attribute of being loved by all the gods. But you still refuse to explain to me the nature of holiness. And therefore, if you please, I will ask you not to hide your treasure, but to tell me once more what holiness or piety really is, whether dear to the gods or not (for that is a matter about which we will not quarrel) and what is impiety?

415   **Euth.** I really do not know, Socrates, how to express what I mean. For somehow or other our arguments, on whatever ground we rest them, seem to turn round and walk away from us.

    Soc. Your words, Euthyphro, are like the handiwork of my ancestor Daedalus; and if I were the sayer or propounder of them,
420 you might say that my arguments walk away and will not remain fixed where they are placed because I am a descendant of his. But now, since these notions are your own, you must find some other gibe, for they certainly, as you yourself allow, show an inclination to be on the move.

425   **Euth.** Nay, Socrates, I shall still say that you are the Daedalus who sets arguments in motion; not I, certainly, but you make them move or go round, for they would never have stirred, as far as I am concerned.

    Soc. Then I must be a greater than Daedalus: for whereas he
430 only made his own inventions to move, I move those of other people as well. And the beauty of it is, that I would rather not. For I would give the wisdom of Daedalus, and the wealth of Tantalus, to be able to detain them and keep them fixed. But enough of this. As I perceive that you are lazy, I will myself endeavor to show you how you might
435 instruct me in the nature of piety; and I hope that you will not grudge your labor. Tell me, then—Is not that which is pious necessarily just?

    Euth. Yes.

    Soc. And is, then, all which is just pious? or, is that which is pious all just, but that which is just, only in part and not all, pious?

440   **Euth.** I do not understand you, Socrates.

    Soc. And yet I know that you are as much wiser than I am, as you are younger. But, as I was saying, revered friend, the abundance of your wisdom makes you lazy. Please to exert yourself, for there is no real difficulty in understanding me. What I mean I may explain by
445 an illustration of what I do not mean. The poet (Stasinus) sings—

    Of Zeus, the author and creator of all these things,

    You will not tell: for where there is fear there is also

    reverence. Now I disagree with this poet. Shall I tell you in what respect?

450   **Euth.** By all means.

    Soc. I should not say that where there is fear there is also reverence; for I am sure that many persons fear poverty and disease, and the like evils, but I do not perceive that they reverence the objects of their fear.

455   **Euth.** Very true.

Soc. But where reverence is, there is fear; for he who has a feeling of reverence and shame about the commission of any action, fears and is afraid of an ill reputation.

Euth. No doubt.

460   **Soc.** Then we are wrong in saying that where there is fear there is also reverence; and we should say, where there is reverence there is also fear. But there is not always reverence where there is fear; for fear is a more extended notion, and reverence is a part of fear, just as the odd is a part of number, and number is a more extended notion

465   than the odd. I suppose that you follow me now?

Euth. Quite well.

Soc. That was the sort of question which I meant to raise when I asked whether the just is always the pious, or the pious always the just; and whether there may not be justice where there is not piety;

470   for justice is the more extended notion of which piety is only a part. Do you dissent?

Euth. No, I think that you are quite right.

Soc. Then, if piety is a part of justice, I suppose that we should inquire what part? If you had pursued the enquiry in the previous

475   cases; for instance, if you had asked me what is an even number, and what part of number the even is, I should have had no difficulty in replying, a number which represents a figure having two equal sides. Do you not agree?

Euth. Yes, I quite agree.

480   **Soc.** In like manner, I want you to tell me what part of justice is piety or holiness, that I may be able to tell Meletus not to do me injustice, or indict me for impiety, as I am now adequately instructed by you in the nature of piety or holiness, and their opposites.

Euth. Piety or holiness, Socrates, appears to me to be that part

485   of justice which attends to the gods, as there is the other part of justice which attends to men.

Soc. That is good, Euthyphro; yet still there is a little point about which I should like to have further information, What is the meaning of "attention"? For attention can hardly be used in the same

490   sense when applied to the gods as when applied to other things. For

instance, horses are said to require attention, and not every person is able to attend to them, but only a person skilled in horsemanship. Is it not so?

Euth. Certainly.

495   **Soc.** I should suppose that the art of horsemanship is the art of attending to horses?

Euth. Yes.

Soc. Nor is every one qualified to attend to dogs, but only the huntsman?

500   **Euth.** True.

Soc. And I should also conceive that the art of the huntsman is the art of attending to dogs?

Euth. Yes.

Soc. As the art of the ox herd is the art of attending to oxen?

505   **Euth.** Very true.

Soc. In like manner holiness or piety is the art of attending to the gods?—that would be your meaning, Euthyphro?

Euth. Yes.

Soc. And is not attention always designed for the good or benefit

510 of that to which the attention is given? As in the case of horses, you may observe that when attended to by the horseman's art they are benefited and improved, are they not?

Euth. True.

Soc. As the dogs are benefited by the huntsman's art, and the

515 oxen by the art of the ox herd, and all other things are tended or attended for their good and not for their hurt?

Euth. Certainly, not for their hurt.

Soc. But for their good?

Euth. Of course.

520   **Soc.** And does piety or holiness, which has been defined to be the art of attending to the gods, benefit or improve them? Would you say that when you do a holy act you make any of the gods better?

Euth. No, no; that was certainly not what I meant.

Soc. And I, Euthyphro, never supposed that you did. I asked you

525 the question about the nature of the attention, because I thought that you did not.

Euth. You do me justice, Socrates; that is not the sort of attention which I mean.

Soc. Good: but I must still ask what is this attention to the gods which is called piety?

Euth. It is such, Socrates, as servants show to their masters.

Soc. I understand—a sort of ministration to the gods.

Euth. Exactly.

Soc. Medicine is also a sort of ministration or service, having in view the attainment of some object—would you not say of health?

Euth. I should.

Soc. Again, there is an art which ministers to the ship-builder with a view to the attainment of some result?

Euth. Yes, Socrates, with a view to the building of a ship.

Soc. As there is an art which ministers to the house builder with a view to the building of a house?

Euth. Yes.

Soc. And now tell me, my good friend, about the art which ministers to the gods: what work does that help to accomplish? For you must surely know if, as you say, you are of all men living the one who is best instructed in religion.

Euth. And I speak the truth, Socrates.

Soc. Tell me then, oh tell me—what is that fair work which the gods do by the help of our ministrations?

Euth. Many and fair, Socrates, are the works which they do.

Soc. Why, my friend, and so are those of a general. But the chief of them is easily told. Would you not say that victory in war is the chief of them?

Euth. Certainly.

Soc. Many and fair, too, are the works of the husbandman, if I am not mistaken; but his chief work is the production of food from the earth?

Euth. Exactly.

Soc. And of the many and fair things done by the gods, which is the chief or principal one?

Euth. I have told you already, Socrates, that to learn all these things accurately will be very tiresome. Let me simply say that piety or holiness is learning, how to please the gods in word and deed, by prayers and sacrifices. Such piety, is the salvation of families and states, just as the impious, which is unpleasing to the gods, is their ruin and destruction.

Soc. I think that you could have answered in much fewer words the chief question which I asked, Euthyphro, if you had chosen. But I see plainly that you are not disposed to instruct me—clearly not: else
570   why, when we reached the point, did you turn, aside? Had you only answered me I should have truly learned of you by this time the nature of piety. Now, as the asker of a question is necessarily dependent on the answerer, whither he leads—I must follow; and can only ask again, what is the pious, and what is piety? Do you
575   mean that they are a, sort of science of praying and sacrificing?

Euth. Yes, I do.

Soc. And sacrificing is giving to the gods, and prayer is asking of the gods?

Euth. Yes, Socrates.

580   **Soc.** Upon this view, then piety is a science of asking and giving?

Euth. You understand me well, Socrates.

Soc. Yes, my friend; the. reason is that I am a votary of your science, and give my mind to it, and therefore nothing which you say will be thrown away upon me. Please then to tell me, what is the
585   nature of this service to the gods? Do you mean that we prefer requests and give gifts to them?

Euth. Yes, I do.

Soc. Is not the right way of asking to ask of them what we want?

Euth. Certainly.

590   **Soc.** And the right way of giving is to give to them in return what they want of us. There would be no, in an art which gives to any one that which he does not want.

Euth. Very true, Socrates.

Soc. Then piety, Euthyphro, is an art which gods and men have
595   of doing business with one another?

Euth. That is an expression which you may use, if you like.

Soc. But I have no particular liking for anything but the truth. I wish, however, that you would tell me what benefit accrues to the gods from our gifts. There is no doubt about what they give to us; for
600   there is no good thing which they do not give; but how we can give any good thing to them in return is far from being equally clear. If they give everything and we give nothing, that must be an affair of business in which we have very greatly the advantage of them.

Euth. And do you imagine, Socrates, that any benefit accrues to
the gods from our gifts?

Soc. But if not, Euthyphro, what is the meaning of gifts which
are conferred by us upon the gods?

Euth. What else, but tributes of honor; and, as I was just now
saying, what pleases them?

Soc. Piety, then, is pleasing to the gods, but not beneficial or
dear to them?

Euth. I should say that nothing could be dearer.

Soc. Then once more the assertion is repeated that piety is dear
to the gods?

Euth. Certainly.

Soc. And when you say this, can you wonder at your words not
standing firm, but walking away? Will you accuse me of being the
Daedalus who makes them walk away, not perceiving that there is
another and far greater artist than Daedalus who makes them go
round in a circle, and he is yourself; for the argument, as you will
perceive, comes round to the same point. Were we not saying that the
holy or pious was not the same with that which is loved of the gods?
Have you forgotten?

Euth. I quite remember.

Soc. And are you not saying that what is loved of the gods is
holy; and is not this the same as what is dear to them—do you see?

Euth. True.

Soc. Then either we were wrong in former assertion; or, if we
were right then, we are wrong now.

Euth. One of the two must be true.

Soc. Then we must begin again and ask, What is piety? That is
an enquiry which I shall never be weary of pursuing as far as in me
lies; and I entreat you not to scorn me, but to apply your mind to the
utmost, and tell me the truth. For, if any man knows, you are he;
and therefore I must detain you, like Proteus, until you tell. If you
had not certainly known the nature of piety and impiety, I am
confident that you would never, on behalf of a serf, have charged your
aged father with murder. You would not have run such a risk of doing
wrong in the sight of the gods, and you would have had too much
respect for the opinions of men. I am sure, therefore, that you know

the nature of piety and impiety. Speak out then, my dear Euthyphro, and do not hide your knowledge.

Euth. Another time, Socrates; for I am in a hurry, and must go now.

645   **Soc.** Alas! my companion, and will you leave me in despair? I was hoping that you would instruct me in the nature of piety and impiety; and then I might have cleared myself of Meletus and his indictment. I would have told him that I had been enlightened by Euthyphro, and had given up rash innovations and speculations, in 650   which I indulged only through ignorance, and that now I am about to lead a better life.

Epicurus, *Letter to Menoeceus*

Greetings.

Let no one be slow to seek wisdom when he is young nor weary in the search for it when he is grown old. For no age is too early or too late for the health of the soul. And to say that the season for
5   studying philosophy has not yet come, or that it is past and gone, is like saying that the season for happiness is not yet or that it is now no more. Therefore, both old and young ought to seek wisdom, the former in order that, as age comes over him, he may be young in good things because of the grace of what has been, and the latter in order
10   that, while he is young, he may at the same time be old, because he has no fear of the things which are to come. So we must exercise ourselves in the things which bring happiness, since, if that be present, we have everything, and, if that be absent, all our actions are directed toward attaining it.

15   Those things which without ceasing I have declared to you, those do, and exercise yourself in those, holding them to be the elements of right life. First believe that God is a living being immortal and happy, according to the notion of a god indicated by the common sense of humankind; and so of him anything that is at agrees not
20   with about him whatever may uphold both his happiness and his immortality. For truly there are gods, and knowledge of them is evident; but they are not such as the multitude believe, seeing that people do not steadfastly maintain the notions they form respecting them. Not the person who denies the gods worshipped by the
25   multitude, but he who affirms of the gods what the multitude believes about them is truly impious. For the utterances of the multitude about the gods are not true preconceptions but false assumptions; hence it is that the greatest evils happen to the wicked and the greatest blessings happen to the good from the hand of the
30   gods, seeing that they are always favorable to their own good qualities and take pleasure in people like to themselves, but reject as alien whatever is not of their kind.

Accustom yourself to believe that death is nothing to us, for good and evil imply awareness, and death is the privation of all
35   awareness; therefore a right understanding that death is nothing to us makes the mortality of life enjoyable, not by adding to life an

unlimited time, but by taking away the yearning after immortality. For life has no terror; for those who thoroughly apprehend that there are no terrors for them in ceasing to live. Foolish, therefore, is the
40 person who says that he fears death, not because it will pain when it comes, but because it pains in the prospect. Whatever causes no annoyance when it is present, causes only a groundless pain in the expectation. Death, therefore, the most awful of evils, is nothing to us, seeing that, when we are, death is not come, and, when death is
45 come, we are not. It is nothing, then, either to the living or to the dead, for with the living it is not and the dead exist no longer. But in the world, at one time people shun death as the greatest of all evils, and at another time choose it as a respite from the evils in life. The wise person does not deprecate life nor does he fear the cessation of
50 life. The thought of life is no offense to him, nor is the cessation of life regarded as an evil. And even as people choose of food not merely and simply the larger portion, but the more pleasant, so the wise seek to enjoy the time which is most pleasant and not merely that which is longest. And he who admonishes the young to live well and the old to
55 make a good end speaks foolishly, not merely because of the desirability of life, but because the same exercise at once teaches to live well and to die well. Much worse is he who says that it were good not to be born, but when once one is born to pass with all speed through the gates of Hades. For if he truly believes this, why does he
60 not depart from life? It were easy for him to do so, if once he were firmly convinced. If he speaks only in mockery, his words are foolishness, for those who hear believe him not.

We must remember that the future is neither wholly ours nor wholly not ours, so that neither must we count upon it as quite
65 certain to come nor despair of it as quite certain not to come.

We must also reflect that of desires some are natural, others are groundless; and that of the natural some are necessary as well as natural, and some natural only. And of the necessary desires some are necessary if we are to be happy, some if the body is to be rid of
70 uneasiness, some if we are even to live. He who has a clear and certain understanding of these things will direct every preference and aversion toward securing health of body and tranquillity of mind, seeing that this is the sum and end of a happy life. For the end of all our actions is to be free from pain and fear, and, when once we have

75 attained all this, the tempest of the soul is laid; seeing that the
living creature has no need to go in search of something that is
lacking, nor to look for anything else by which the good of the soul
and of the body will be fulfilled. When we are pained, then, and then
only, do we feel the need of pleasure. For this reason we call pleasure
80 the alpha and omega of a happy life. Pleasure is our first and
kindred good. It is the starting-point of every choice and of every
aversion, and to it we come back, inasmuch as we make feeling the
rule by which to judge of every good thing. And since pleasure is our
first and native good, for that reason we do not choose every pleasure
85 whatever, but often pass over many pleasures when a greater
annoyance ensues from them. And often we consider pains superior
to pleasures when submission to the pains for a long time brings us
as a consequence a greater pleasure. While therefore all pleasure
because it is naturally akin to us is good, not all pleasure is worthy
90 of choice, just as all pain is an evil and yet not all pain is to be
shunned. It is, however, by measuring one against another, and by
looking at the conveniences and inconveniences, teat all these
matters must be judged. Sometimes we treat the good as an evil,
and the evil, on the contrary, as a good. Again, we regard.
95 independence of outward things as a great good, not so as in all
cases to use little, but so as to be contented with little if we have not
much, being honestly persuaded that they have the sweetest
enjoyment of luxury who stand least in need of it, and that whatever
is natural is easily procured and only the vain and worthless hard to
100 win. Plain fare gives as much pleasure as a costly diet, when one the
pain of want has been removed, while bread an water confer the
highest possible pleasure when they are brought to hungry lips. To
habituate one's se therefore, to simple and inexpensive diet supplies
al that is needful for health, and enables a person to meet the
105 necessary requirements of life without shrinking and it places us in a
better condition when we approach at intervals a costly fare and
renders us fearless of fortune.

When we say, then, that pleasure is the end and aim, we do not
mean the pleasures of the prodigal or the pleasures of sensuality, as
110 we are understood to do by some through ignorance, prejudice, or
willful misrepresentation. By pleasure we mean the absence of pain
in the body and of trouble in the soul. It is not an unbroken

succession of drinking-bouts and of merrymaking, not sexual love, not
the enjoyment of the fish and other delicacies of a luxurious table,
115   which produce a pleasant life; it is sober reasoning, searching out the
grounds of every choice and avoidance, and banishing those beliefs
through which the greatest disturbances take possession of the soul.
Of all this the d is prudence. For this reason prudence is a more
precious thing even than the other virtues, for ad a life of pleasure
120   which is not also a life of prudence, honor, and justice; nor lead a life
of prudence, honor, and justice, which is not also a life of pleasure.
For the virtues have grown into one with a pleasant life, and a
pleasant life is inseparable from them.

Who, then, is superior in your judgment to such a person? He
125   holds a holy belief concerning the gods, and is altogether free from the
fear of death. He has diligently considered the end fixed by nature,
and understands how easily the limit of good things can be reached
and attained, and how either the duration or the intensity of evils is
but slight. Destiny which some introduce as sovereign over all things,
130   he laughs to scorn, affirming rather that some things happen of
necessity, others by chance, others through our own agency. For he
sees that necessity destroys responsibility and that chance or fortune
is inconstant; whereas our own actions are free, and it is to them
that praise and blame naturally attach. It were better, indeed, to
135   accept the legends of the gods than to bow beneath destiny which the
natural philosophers have imposed. The one holds out some faint
hope that we may escape if we honor the gods, while the necessity of
the naturalists is deaf to all entreaties. Nor does he hold chance to
be a god, as the world in general does, for in the acts of a god there is
140   no disorder; nor to be a cause, though an uncertain one, for he
believes that no good or evil is dispensed by chance to people so as to
make life happy, though it supplies the starting-point of great good
and great evil. He believes that the misfortune of the wise is better
than the prosperity of the fool. It is better, in short, that what is well
145   judged in action should not owe its successful issue to the aid of
chance.

Exercise yourself in these and kindred precepts day and night,
both by yourself and with him who is like to you; then never, either in
waking or in dream, will you be disturbed, but will live as a god

150   among people. For people lose all appearance of mortality by living in the midst of immortal blessings.

Epictetus, *Enchiridion*

1. Some things are in our control and others not. Things in our control are opinion, pursuit, desire, aversion, and, in a word, whatever are our own actions. Things not in our control are body, property, reputation, command, and, in one word, whatever are not
5 our own actions.

The things in our control are by nature free, unrestrained, unhindered; but those not in our control are weak, slavish, restrained, belonging to others. Remember, then, that if you suppose that things which are slavish by nature are also free, and that what
10 belongs to others is your own, then you will be hindered. You will lament, you will be disturbed, and you will find fault both with gods and men. But if you suppose that only to be your own which is your own, and what belongs to others such as it really is, then no one will ever compel you or restrain you. Further, you will find fault with no
15 one or accuse no one. You will do nothing against your will. No one will hurt you, you will have no enemies, and you not be harmed.

Aiming therefore at such great things, remember that you must not allow yourself to be carried, even with a slight tendency, towards the attainment of lesser things. Instead, you must entirely quit some
20 things and for the present postpone the rest. But if you would both have these great things, along with power and riches, then you will not gain even the latter, because you aim at the former too: but you will absolutely fail of the former, by which alone happiness and freedom are achieved.

25 Work, therefore to be able to say to every harsh appearance, "You are but an appearance, and not absolutely the thing you appear to be." And then examine it by those rules which you have, and first, and chiefly, by this: whether it concerns the things which are in our own control, or those which are not; and, if it concerns anything not in
30 our control, be prepared to say that it is nothing to you.

2. Remember that following desire promises the attainment of that of which you are desirous; and aversion promises the avoiding that to which you are averse. However, he who fails to obtain the object of his desire is disappointed, and he who incurs the object of
35 his aversion wretched. If, then, you confine your aversion to those objects only which are contrary to the natural use of your faculties,

which you have in your own control, you will never incur anything to
which you are averse. But if you are averse to sickness, or death, or
poverty, you will be wretched. Remove aversion, then, from all things
40   that are not in our control, and transfer it to things contrary to the
nature of what is in our control. But, for the present, totally suppress
desire: for, if you desire any of the things which are not in your own
control, you must necessarily be disappointed; and of those which
are, and which it would be laudable to desire, nothing is yet in your
45   possession. Use only the appropriate actions of pursuit and
avoidance; and even these lightly, and with gentleness and
reservation.

3. With regard to whatever objects give you delight, are useful, or
are deeply loved, remember to tell yourself of what general nature
50   they are, beginning from the most insignificant things. If, for
example, you are fond of a specific ceramic cup, remind yourself that
it is only ceramic cups in general of which you are fond. Then, if it
breaks, you will not be disturbed. If you kiss your child, or your wife,
say that you only kiss things which are human, and thus you will not
55   be disturbed if either of them dies.

4. When you are going about any action, remind yourself what
nature the action is. If you are going to bathe, picture to yourself the
things which usually happen in the bath: some people splash the
water, some push, some use abusive language, and others steal.
60   Thus you will more safely go about this action if you say to yourself,
"I will now go bathe, and keep my own mind in a state conformable
to nature." And in the same manner with regard to every other
action. For thus, if any hindrance arises in bathing, you will have it
ready to say, "It was not only to bathe that I desired, but to keep my
65   mind in a state conformable to nature; and I will not keep it if I am
bothered at things that happen.

5. Men are disturbed, not by things, but by the principles and
notions which they form concerning things. Death, for instance, is not
terrible, else it would have appeared so to Socrates. But the terror
70   consists in our notion of death that it is terrible. When therefore we
are hindered, or disturbed, or grieved, let us never attribute it to
others, but to ourselves; that is, to our own principles. An
uninstructed person will lay the fault of his own bad condition upon
others. Someone just starting instruction will lay the fault on himself.

75   Some who is perfectly instructed will place blame neither on others
      nor on himself.

      6. Don't be prideful with any excellence that is not your own. If a
      horse should be prideful and say, " I am handsome," it would be
      supportable. But when you are prideful, and say, " I have a
80   handsome horse," know that you are proud of what is, in fact, only
      the good of the horse. What, then, is your own? Only your reaction to
      the appearances of things. Thus, when you behave conformably to
      nature in reaction to how things appear, you will be proud with
      reason; for you will take pride in some good of your own.

85   7. Consider when, on a voyage, your ship is anchored; if you go on
      shore to get water you may along the way amuse yourself with
      picking up a shellfish, or an onion. However, your thoughts and
      continual attention ought to be bent towards the ship, waiting for the
      captain to call on board; you must then immediately leave all these
90   things, otherwise you will be thrown into the ship, bound neck and
      feet like a sheep. So it is with life. If, instead of an onion or a
      shellfish, you are given a wife or child, that is fine. But if the captain
      calls, you must run to the ship, leaving them, and regarding none of
      them. But if you are old, never go far from the ship: lest, when you
95   are called, you should be unable to come in time.

      8. Don't demand that things happen as you wish, but wish that
      they happen as they do happen, and you will go on well.

      9. Sickness is a hindrance to the body, but not to your ability to
      choose, unless that is your choice. Lameness is a hindrance to the
100   leg, but not to your ability to choose. Say this to yourself with regard
      to everything that happens, then you will see such obstacles as
      hindrances to something else, but not to yourself.

      10. With every accident, ask yourself what abilities you have for
      making a proper use of it. If you see an attractive person, you will
105   find that self-restraint is the ability you have against your desire. If
      you are in pain, you will find fortitude. If you hear unpleasant
      language, you will find patience. And thus habituated, the
      appearances of things will not hurry you away along with them.

      11. Never say of anything, "I have lost it"; but, "I have returned
110   it." Is your child dead? It is returned. Is your wife dead? She is
      returned. Is your estate taken away? Well, and is not that likewise
      returned? "But he who took it away is a bad man." What difference is

it to you who the giver assigns to take it back? While he gives it to
you to possess, take care of it; but don't view it as your own, just as
115   travelers view a hotel.

12. If you want to improve, reject such arguments as these: "If I
neglect my affairs, I'll have no income; if I don't correct my servant, he
will be bad." For it is better to die with hunger, exempt from grief
and fear, than to live in affluence with perturbation; and it is better
120   your servant should be bad, than you unhappy.

Begin therefore from little things. Is a little oil spilt? A little wine
stolen? Say to yourself, "This is the price paid for apathy, for
tranquillity, and nothing is to be had for nothing." When you call your
servant, it is possible that he may not come; or, if he does, he may
125   not do what you want. But he is by no means of such importance
that it should be in his power to give you any disturbance.

13. If you want to improve, be content to be thought foolish and
stupid with regard to external things. Don't wish to be thought to
know anything; and even if you appear to be somebody important to
130   others, distrust yourself. For, it is difficult to both keep your faculty of
choice in a state conformable to nature, and at the same time acquire
external things. But while you are careful about the one, you must of
necessity neglect the other.

14. If you wish your children, and your wife, and your friends to
135   live for ever, you are stupid; for you wish to be in control of things
which you cannot, you wish for things that belong to others to be your
own. So likewise, if you wish your servant to be without fault, you are
a fool; for you wish vice not to be vice," but something else. But, if you
wish to have your desires fulfilled, this is in your own control.
140   Exercise, therefore, what is in your control. He is the master of every
other person who is able to confer or remove whatever that person
wishes either to have or to avoid. Whoever, then, would be free, let
him wish nothing, let him decline nothing, which depends on others
else he must necessarily be a slave.

145   15. Remember that you must behave in life as at a dinner party.
Is anything brought around to you? Put out your hand and take your
share with moderation. Does it pass by you? Don't stop it. Is it not
yet come? Don't stretch your desire towards it, but wait till it reaches
you. Do this with regard to children, to a wife, to public posts, to
150   riches, and you will eventually be a worthy partner of the feasts of

the gods. And if you don't even take the things which are set before you, but are able even to reject them, then you will not only be a partner at the feasts of the gods, but also of their empire. For, by doing this, Diogenes, Heraclitus and others like them, deservedly became, and were called, divine.

16. When you see anyone weeping in grief because his son has gone abroad, or is dead, or because he has suffered in his affairs, be careful that the appearance may not misdirect you. Instead, distinguish within your own mind, and be prepared to say, "It's not the accident that distresses this person., because it doesn't distress another person; it is the judgment which he makes about it." As far as words go, however, don't reduce yourself to his level, and certainly do not moan with him. Do not moan inwardly either.

17. Remember that you are an actor in a drama, of such a kind as the author pleases to make it. If short, of a short one; if long, of a long one. If it is his pleasure you should act a poor man, a cripple, a governor, or a private person, see that you act it naturally. For this is your business, to act well the character assigned you; to choose it is another's.

18. When a raven happens to croak unluckily, don't allow the appearance hurry you away with it, but immediately make the distinction to yourself, and say, "None of these things are foretold to me; but either to my paltry body, or property, or reputation, or children, or wife. But to me all omens are lucky, if I will. For whichever of these things happens, it is in my control to derive advantage from it."

19. You may be unconquerable, if you enter into no combat in which it is not in your own control to conquer. When, therefore, you see anyone eminent in honors, or power, or in high esteem on any other account, take heed not to be hurried away with the appearance, and to pronounce him happy; for, if the essence of good consists in things in our own control, there will be no room for envy or emulation. But, for your part, don't wish to be a general, or a senator, or a consul, but to be free; and the only way to this is a contempt of things not in our own control.

20. Remember, that not he who gives ill language or a blow insults, but the principle which represents these things as insulting. When, therefore, anyone provokes you, be assured that it is your own

opinion which provokes you. Try, therefore, in the first place, not to
190   be hurried away with the appearance. For if you once gain time and
respite, you will more easily command yourself.

21. Let death and exile, and all other things which appear
terrible be daily before your eyes, but chiefly death, and you win
never entertain any abject thought, nor too eagerly covet anything.

195   22. If you have an earnest desire of attaining to philosophy,
prepare yourself from the very first to be laughed at, to be sneered by
the multitude, to hear them say,." He is returned to us a philosopher
all at once," and " Whence this supercilious look?" Now, for your part,
don't have a supercilious look indeed; but keep steadily to those
200   things which appear best to you as one appointed by God to this
station. For remember that, if you adhere to the same point, those
very persons who at first ridiculed will afterwards admire you. But if
you are conquered by them, you will incur a double ridicule.

23. If you ever happen to turn your attention to externals, so as
205   to wish to please anyone, be assured that you have ruined your
scheme of life. Be contented, then, in everything with being a
philosopher; and, if you wish to be thought so likewise by anyone,
appear so to yourself, and it will suffice you.

24. Don't allow such considerations as these distress you. "I will
210   live in dishonor, and be nobody anywhere." For, if dishonor is an evil,
you can no more be involved in any evil by the means of another,
than be engaged in anything base. Is it any business of yours, then,
to get power, or to be admitted to an entertainment? By no means.
How, then, after all, is this a dishonor? And how is it true that you
215   will be nobody anywhere, when you ought to be somebody in those
things only which are in your own control, in which you may be of the
greatest consequence? "But my friends will be unassisted." — What
do you mean by unassisted? They will not have money from you, nor
will you make them Roman citizens. Who told you, then, that these
220   are among the things in our own control, and not the affair of others?
And who can give to another the things which he has not himself?
"Well, but get them, then, that we too may have a share." If I can get
them with the preservation of my own honor and fidelity and
greatness of mind, show me the way and I will get them; but if you
225   require me to lose my own proper good that you may gain what is not
good, consider how inequitable and foolish you are. Besides, which

would you rather have, a sum of money, or a friend of fidelity and
honor? Rather assist me, then, to gain this character than require me
to do those things by which I may lose it. Well, but my country, say
230   you, as far as depends on me, will be unassisted. Here again, what
assistance is this you mean? "It will not have porticoes nor baths of
your providing." And what signifies that? Why, neither does a smith
provide it with shoes, or a shoemaker with arms. It is enough if
everyone fully performs his own proper business. And were you to
235   supply it with another citizen of honor and fidelity, would not he be of
use to it? Yes. Therefore neither are you yourself useless to it. "What
place, then, say you, will I hold in the state?" Whatever you can hold
with the preservation of your fidelity and honor. But if, by desiring to
be useful to that, you lose these, of what use can you be to your
240   country when you are become faithless and void of shame.

25. Is anyone preferred before you at an entertainment, or in a
compliment, or in being admitted to a consultation? If these things
are good, you ought to be glad that he has gotten them; and if they
are evil, don't be grieved that you have not gotten them. And
245   remember that you cannot, without using the same means [which
others do] to acquire things not in our own control, expect to be
thought worthy of an equal share of them. For how can he who does
not frequent the door of any [great] man, does not attend him, does
not praise him, have an equal share with him who does? You are
250   unjust, then, and insatiable, if you are unwilling to pay the price for
which these things are sold, and would have them for nothing. For
how much is lettuce sold? Fifty cents, for instance. If another, then,
paying fifty cents, takes the lettuce, and you, not paying it, go
without them, don't imagine that he has gained any advantage over
255   you. For as he has the lettuce, so you have the fifty cents which you
did not give. So, in the present case, you have not been invited to
such a person's entertainment, because you have not paid him the
price for which a supper is sold. It is sold for praise; it is sold for
attendance. Give him then the value, if it is for your advantage. But
260   if you would, at the same time, not pay the one and yet receive the
other, you are insatiable, and a blockhead. Have you nothing, then,
instead of the supper? Yes, indeed, you have: the not praising him,
whom you don't like to praise; the not bearing with his behavior at
coming in.

265   26. The will of nature may be learned from those things in which we don't distinguish from each other. For example, when our neighbor's boy breaks a cup, or the like, we are presently ready to say, "These things will happen." Be assured, then, that when your own cup likewise is broken, you ought to be affected just as when

270   another's cup was broken. Apply this in like manner to greater things. Is the child or wife of another dead? There is no one who would not say, "This is a human accident." but if anyone's own child happens to die, it is presently, "Alas I how wretched am I!" But it should be remembered how we are affected in hearing the same thing

275   concerning others.

27. As a mark is not set up for the sake of missing the aim, so neither does the nature of evil exist in the world.

28. If a person gave your body to any stranger he met on his way, you would certainly be angry. And do you feel no shame in handing

280   over your own mind to be confused and mystified by anyone who happens to verbally attack you?

29. In every affair consider what precedes and follows, and then undertake it. Otherwise you will begin with spirit; but not having thought of the consequences, when some of them appear you will

285   shamefully desist. "I would conquer at the Olympic games." But consider what precedes and follows, and then, if it is for your advantage, engage in the affair. You must conform to rules, submit to a diet, refrain from dainties; exercise your body, whether you choose it or not, at a stated hour, in heat and cold; you must drink no cold

290   water, nor sometimes even wine. In a word, you must give yourself up to your master, as to a physician. Then, in the combat, you may be thrown into a ditch, dislocate your arm, turn your ankle, swallow dust, be whipped, and, after all, lose the victory. When you have evaluated all this, if your inclination still holds, then go to war.

295   Otherwise, take notice, you will behave like children who sometimes play like wrestlers, sometimes gladiators, sometimes blow a trumpet, and sometimes act a tragedy when they have seen and admired these shows. Thus you too will be at one time a wrestler, at another a gladiator, now a philosopher, then an orator; but with your

300   whole soul, nothing at all. Like an ape, you mimic all you see, and one thing after another is sure to please you, but is out of favor as soon as it becomes familiar. For you have never entered upon

anything considerately, nor after having viewed the whole matter on all sides, or made any scrutiny into it, but rashly, and with a cold
305 inclination. Thus some, when they have seen a philosopher and heard a man speaking like Euphrates (though, indeed, who can speak like him?), have a mind to be philosophers too. Consider first, man, what the matter is, and what your own nature is able to bear. If you would be a wrestler, consider your shoulders, your back, your
310 thighs; for different persons are made for different things. Do you think that you can act as you do, and be a philosopher? That you can eat and drink, and be angry and discontented as you are now? You must watch, you must labor, you must get the better of certain appetites, must quit your acquaintance, be despised by your servant,
315 be laughed at by those you meet; come off worse than others in everything, in magistracies, in honors, in courts of judicature. When you have considered all these things round, approach, if you please; if, by parting with them, you have a mind to purchase apathy, freedom, and tranquillity. If not, don't come here; don't, like children,
320 be one while a philosopher, then a publican, then an orator, and then one of Caesar's officers. These things are not consistent. You must be one man, either good or bad. You must cultivate either your own ruling faculty or externals, and apply yourself either to things within or without you; that is, be either a philosopher, or one of the vulgar.
325   30. Duties are universally measured by relations. Is anyone a father? If so, it is implied that the children should take care of him, submit to him in everything, patiently listen to his reproaches, his correction. But he is a bad father. Are you naturally entitled, then, to a good father? No, only to a father. Is a brother unjust? Well, keep
330 your own situation towards him. Consider not what he does, but what you are to do to keep your own faculty of choice in a state conformable to nature. For another will not hurt you unless you please. You will then be hurt when you think you are hurt. In this manner, therefore, you will find, from the idea of a neighbor, a
335 citizen, a general, the corresponding duties if you accustom yourself to contemplate the several relations.
    31. Be assured that the essential property of piety towards the gods is to form right opinions concerning them, as existing "I and as governing the universe with goodness and justice. And fix yourself in
340 this resolution, to obey them, and yield to them, and willingly follow

them in all events, as produced by the most perfect understanding. For thus you will never find fault with the gods, nor accuse them as neglecting you. And it is not possible for this to be effected any other way than by withdrawing yourself from things not in our own control, and placing good or evil in those only which are. For if you suppose any of the things not in our own control to be either good or evil, when you are disappointed of what you wish, or incur what you would avoid, you must necessarily find fault with and blame the authors. For every animal is naturally formed to fly and abhor things that appear hurtful, and the causes of them; and to pursue and admire those which appear beneficial, and the causes of them. It is impractical, then, that one who supposes himself to be hurt should be happy about the person who, he thinks, hurts him, just as it is impossible to be happy about the hurt itself. Hence, also, a father is reviled by a son, when he does not impart to him the things which he takes to be good; and the supposing empire to be a good made Polynices and Eteocles mutually enemies. On this account the farmer, the sailor, the merchant, on this account those who lose wives and children, revile the gods. For where interest is, there too is piety placed. So that, whoever is careful to regulate his desires and aversions as he ought, is, by the very same means, careful of piety likewise. But it is also incumbent on everyone to offer libations and sacrifices and first fruits, conformably to the customs of his country, with purity, and not in a slovenly manner, nor negligently, nor sparingly, nor beyond his ability.

32. When you have recourse to divination, remember that you know not what the event will be, and you come to learn it of the diviner; but of what nature it is you know before you come, at least if you are a philosopher. For if it is among the things not in our own control, it can by no means be either good or evil. Don't, therefore, bring either desire or aversion with you to the diviner (else you will approach him trembling), but first acquire a distinct knowledge that every event is indifferent and nothing to you., of whatever sort it may be, for it will be in your power to make a right use of it, and this no one can hinder; then come with confidence to the gods, as your counselors, and afterwards, when any counsel is given you, remember what counselors you have assumed, and whose advice you will neglect if you disobey. Come to divination, as Socrates prescribed, in

cases of which the whole consideration relates to the event, and in
which no opportunities are afforded by reason, or any other art, to
discover the thing proposed to be learned. When, therefore, it is our
duty to share the danger of a friend or of our country, we ought not to
consult the oracle whether we will share it with them or not. For,
though the diviner should forewarn you that the victims are
unfavorable, this means no more than that either death or
mutilation or exile is portended. But we have reason within us, and
it directs, even with these hazards, to the greater diviner, the
Pythian god, who cast out of the temple the person who gave no
assistance to his friend while another was murdering him.

33. Immediately prescribe some character and form of conduct to
yourself, which you may keep both alone and in company.

Be for the most part silent, or speak merely what is necessary,
and in few words. We may, however, enter, though sparingly, into
discourse sometimes when occasion calls for it, but not on any of the
common subjects, of gladiators, or horse races, or athletic champions,
or feasts, the vulgar topics of conversation; but principally not of men,
so as either to blame, or praise, or make comparisons. If you are
able, then, by your own conversation bring over that of your company
to proper subjects; but, if you happen to be taken among strangers,
be silent.

Don't allow your laughter be much, nor on many occasions, nor
profuse.

Avoid swearing, if possible, altogether; if not, as far as you are
able.

Avoid public and vulgar entertainment; but, if ever an occasion
calls you to them, keep your attention upon the stretch, that you may
not imperceptibly slide into vulgar manners. For be assured that if a
person be ever so sound himself, yet, if his companion be infected, he
who converses with him will be infected likewise.

Provide things relating to the body no further than mere use; as
meat, drink, clothing, house, family. But strike off and reject
everything relating to show and delicacy.

As far as possible, before marriage, keep yourself pure from
familiarities with women, and, if you indulge them, let it be
lawfully." But don't therefore be troublesome and full of reproofs to

those who use these liberties, nor frequently boast that you yourself don't.

If anyone tells you that such a person speaks ill of you, don't make excuses about what is said of you, but answer: " He does not
420 know my other faults, else he would not have mentioned only these."

It is not necessary for you to appear often at public spectacles; but if ever there is a proper occasion for you to be there, don't appear more solicitous for anyone than for yourself; that is, wish things to be only just as they are, and him only to conquer who is the conqueror,
425 for thus you will meet with no hindrance. But abstain entirely from declamations and derision and violent emotions. And when you come away, don't discourse a great deal on what has passed, and what does not contribute to your own amendment. For it would appear by such discourse that you were immoderately struck with the show.
430 Go not [of your own accord] to the rehearsals of any [authors], nor appear [at them] readily. But, if you do appear, keep your gravity and dignity, and at the same time avoid being morose.

When you are going to confer with anyone, and particularly of those in a superior station, represent to yourself how Socrates or
435 Zeno would behave in such a case, and you will not be at a loss to make a proper use of whatever may occur.

When you are going to any of the people in power, represent to yourself that you will not find him at home; that you will not be admitted; that the doors will not be opened to you; that he will take
440 no notice of you. If, with all this, it is your duty to go, bear what happens, and never say [to yourself], " It was not worth so much." For this is vulgar, and like a man dazed by external things.

In parties of conversation, avoid a frequent and excessive mention of your own actions and dangers. For, however agreeable it
445 may be to yourself to mention the risks you have run, it is not equally agreeable to others to hear your adventures. Avoid, likewise, an endeavor to excite laughter. For this is a slippery point, which may throw you into vulgar manners, and, besides, may be apt to lessen you in the esteem of your acquaintance. Approaches to indecent
450 discourse are likewise dangerous. Whenever, therefore, anything of this sort happens, if there be a proper opportunity, rebuke him who makes advances that way; or, at least, by silence and blushing and a forbidding look, show yourself to be displeased by such talk.

34. If you are struck by the appearance of any promised pleasure, guard yourself against being hurried away by it; but let the affair wait your leisure, and procure yourself some delay. Then bring to your mind both points of time: that in which you will enjoy the pleasure, and that in which you will repent and reproach yourself after you have enjoyed it; and set before you, in opposition to these, how you will be glad and applaud yourself if you abstain. And even though it should appear to you a seasonable gratification, take heed that its enticing, and agreeable and attractive force may not subdue you; but set in opposition to this how much better it is to be conscious of having gained so great a victory.

35. When you do anything from a clear judgment that it ought to be done, never shun the being seen to do it, even though the world should make a wrong supposition about it; for, if you don't act right, shun the action itself; but, if you do, why are you afraid of those who censure you wrongly?

36. As the proposition, "Either it is day or it is night," is extremely proper for a disjunctive argument, but quite improper in a conjunctive one, so, at a feast, to choose the largest share is very suitable to the bodily appetite, but utterly inconsistent with the social spirit of an entertainment. When you eat with another, then, remember not only the value of those things which are set before you to the body, but the value of that behavior which ought to be observed towards the person who gives the entertainment.

37. If you have assumed any character above your strength, you have both made an ill figure in that and quitted one which you might have supported.

38. When walking, you are careful not to step on a nail or turn your foot; so likewise be careful not to hurt the ruling faculty of your mind. And, if we were to guard against this in every action, we should undertake the action with the greater safety.

39. The body is to everyone the measure of the possessions proper for it, just as the foot is of the shoe. If, therefore, you stop at this, you will keep the measure; but if you move beyond it, you must necessarily be carried forward, as down a cliff; as in the case of a shoe, if you go beyond its fitness to the foot, it comes first to be gilded, then purple, and then studded with jewels. For to that which once exceeds a due measure, there is no bound.

40. Women from fourteen years old are flattered with the title of "mistresses" by the men. Therefore, perceiving that they are regarded only as qualified to give the men pleasure, they begin to adorn

495   themselves, and in that to place ill their hopes. We should, therefore, fix our attention on making them sensible that they are valued for the appearance of decent, modest and discreet behavior.

41. It is a mark of want of genius to spend much time in things relating to the body, as to be long in our exercises, in eating and

500   drinking, and in the discharge of other animal functions. These should be done incidentally and slightly, and our whole attention be engaged in the care of the understanding.

42. When any person harms you, or speaks badly of you, remember that he acts or speaks from a supposition of its being his

505   duty. Now, it is not possible that he should follow what appears right to you, but what appears so to himself. Therefore, if he judges from a wrong appearance, he is the person hurt, since he too is the person deceived. For if anyone should suppose a true proposition to be false, the proposition is not hurt, but he who is deceived about it.

510   Setting out, then, from these principles, you will meekly bear a person who reviles you, for you will say upon every occasion, "It seemed so to him."

43. Everything has two handles, the one by which it may be carried, the other by which it cannot. If your brother acts unjustly,

515   don't lay hold on the action by the handle of his injustice, for by that it cannot be carried; but by the opposite, that he is your brother, that he was brought up with you; and thus you will lay hold on it, as it is to be carried.

44. These arguments are unconnected: "I am richer than you,

520   therefore I am better"; "I am more eloquent than you, therefore I am better." The connection is rather this: "I am richer than you, therefore my property is greater than yours;" "I am more eloquent than you, therefore my style is better than yours." But you, after all, are neither property nor style.

525   45. Does anyone bathe in a mighty little time? Don't say that he does it ill, but in a mighty little time. Does anyone drink a great quantity of wine? Don't say that he does ill, but that he drinks a great quantity. For, unless you perfectly understand the principle from which anyone acts, how should you know if he acts ill? Thus you

530   will not run the hazard of assenting to any appearances but such as
      you fully comprehend.

      46. Never call yourself a philosopher, nor talk a great deal among
      the unlearned about theorems, but act conformably to them. Thus, at
      an entertainment, don't talk how persons ought to eat, but eat as
535   you ought. For remember that in this manner Socrates also
      universally avoided all ostentation. And when persons came to him
      and desired to be recommended by him to philosophers, he took and
      recommended them, so well did he bear being overlooked. So that if
      ever any talk should happen among the unlearned concerning
540   philosophic theorems, be you, for the most part, silent. For there is
      great danger in immediately throwing out what you have not
      digested. And, if anyone tells you that you know nothing, and you are
      not nettled at it, then you may be sure that you have begun your
      business. For sheep don't throw up the grass to show the shepherds
545   how much they have eaten; but, inwardly digesting their food, they
      outwardly produce wool and milk. Thus, therefore, do you likewise
      not show theorems to the unlearned, but the actions produced by
      them after they have been digested.

      47. When you have brought yourself to supply the necessities of
550   your body at a small price, don't pique yourself upon it; nor, if you
      drink water, be saying upon every occasion, "I drink water." But first
      consider how much more sparing and patient of hardship the poor
      are than we. But if at any time you would inure yourself by exercise
      to labor, and bearing hard trials, do it for your own sake, and not for
555   the world; don't grasp statues, but, when you are violently thirsty,
      take a little cold water in your mouth, and spurt it out and tell
      nobody.

      48. The condition and characteristic of a vulgar person, is, that
      he never expects either benefit or hurt from himself, but from
560   externals. The condition and characteristic of a philosopher is, that
      he expects all hurt and benefit from himself. The marks of a
      proficient are, that he censures no one, praises no one, blames no
      one, accuses no one, says nothing concerning himself as being
      anybody, or knowing anything: when he is, in any instance, hindered
565   or restrained, he accuses himself; and, if he is praised, he secretly
      laughs at the person who praises him; and, if he is censured, he
      makes no defense. But he goes about with the caution of sick or

injured people, dreading to move anything that is set right, before it
is perfectly fixed. He suppresses all desire in himself; he transfers his
570   aversion to those things only which thwart the proper use of our own
faculty of choice; the exertion of his active powers towards anything is
very gentle; if he appears stupid or ignorant, he does not care, and, in
a word, he watches himself as an enemy, and one in ambush.

49. When anyone shows himself overly confident in ability to
575   understand and interpret the works of Chrysippus, say to yourself, "
Unless Chrysippus had written obscurely, this person would have
had no subject for his vanity. But what do I desire? To understand
nature and follow her. I ask, then, who interprets her, and, finding
Chrysippus does, I have recourse to him. I don't understand his
580   writings. I seek, therefore, one to interpret them." So far there is
nothing to value myself upon. And when I find an interpreter, what
remains is to make use of his instructions. This alone is the valuable
thing. But, if I admire nothing but merely the interpretation, what do
I become more than a grammarian instead of a philosopher? Except,
585   indeed, that instead of Homer I interpret Chrysippus. When anyone,
therefore, desires me to read Chrysippus to him, I rather blush when
I cannot show my actions agreeable and consonant to his discourse.

50. Whatever moral rules you have deliberately proposed to
yourself. abide by them as they were laws, and as if you would be
590   guilty of impiety by violating any of them. Don't regard what anyone
says of you, for this, after all, is no concern of yours. How long, then,
will you put off thinking yourself worthy of the highest improvements
and   follow   the   distinctions   of   reason?   You   have   received   the
philosophical theorems, with which you ought to be familiar, and you
595   have been familiar with them. What other master, then, do you wait
for, to throw upon that the delay of reforming yourself? You are no
longer a boy, but a grown man. If, therefore, you will be negligent and
slothful, and always add procrastination to procrastination, purpose
to purpose, and fix day after day in which you will attend to yourself,
600   you will insensibly continue without proficiency, and, living and
dying, persevere in being one of the vulgar. This instant, then, think
yourself worthy of living as a man grown up, and a proficient. Let
whatever appears to be the best be to you an inviolable law. And if
any instance of pain or pleasure, or glory or disgrace, is set before
605   you, remember that now is the combat, now the Olympiad comes on,

nor can it be put off. By once being defeated and giving way, proficiency is lost, or by the contrary preserved. Thus Socrates became perfect, improving himself by everything. attending to nothing but reason. And though you are not yet a Socrates, you ought, however, to live as one desirous of becoming a Socrates.

51. The first and most necessary topic in philosophy is that of the use of moral theorems, such as, "We ought not to lie;" the second is that of demonstrations, such as, "What is the origin of our obligation not to lie;" the third gives strength and articulation to the other two, such as, "What is the origin of this is a demonstration." For what is demonstration? What is consequence? What contradiction? What truth? What falsehood? The third topic, then, is necessary on the account of the second, and the second on the account of the first. But the most necessary, and that whereon we ought to rest, is the first. But we act just on the contrary. For we spend all our time on the third topic, and employ all our diligence about that, and entirely neglect the first. Therefore, at the same time that we lie, we are immediately prepared to show how it is demonstrated that lying is not right.

52. Upon all occasions we ought to have these maxims ready at hand:

Conduct me, Jove, and you, 0 Destiny,

Wherever your decrees have fixed my station.

I follow cheerfully; and, did I not,

Wicked and wretched, I must follow still.

Whoever yields properly to Fate, is deemed

Wise among men, and knows the laws of heaven.

And this third:

O Crito, if it thus pleases the gods, thus let it be. Anytus and Melitus may kill me indeed, but hurt me they cannot.

Augustine of Hippo, *The City of God*

BOOK XIX

CHAPTER I—That Varro has made out that two hundred and eighty-eight different sects of philosophy might be formed by the various opinions regarding the supreme good.

As I see that I have still to discuss the fit destinies of the two cities, the earthly and the heavenly, I must first explain, so far as the limits of this work allow me, the reasoning by which men have attempted to make for themselves a happiness in this unhappy life,
5 in order that it may be evident, not only from divine authority, but also from such reasons as can be adduced to unbelievers, how the empty dreams of the philosophers differ from the hope which God gives to us, and from the substantial fulfillment of it which He will give us as our blessedness. Philosophers have expressed a great
10 variety of, diverse opinions regarding the ends of goods and of evils, and this question they have eagerly canvassed, that they might, if possible, discover what makes a man happy. For the end of our good is that for the sake of which other things are to be desired, while it is to be desired for its own sake; and the end of evil is that on account
15 of which other things are to be shunned, while it is avoided on its own account. Thus, by the end of good, we at present mean, not that by which good is destroyed, so that it no longer exists, but that by which it is finished, so that it becomes complete; and by the end of evil we mean, not that which abolishes it, but that which completes
20 its development.

These two ends, therefore, are the supreme good and the supreme evil; and, as I have said, those who have in this vain life professed the study of wisdom have been at great pains to discover these ends, and to obtain the supreme good and avoid the supreme
25 evil in this life. And although they erred in a variety of ways, yet natural insight has prevented them from wandering from the truth so far that they have not placed the supreme good and evil, some in the soul, some in the body, and some in both. ...

43

Chapter III: Which of the three leading opinions regarding the
30 chief good should be preferred, according to Varro, who follows
Antiochus and the Old Academy.

Which of these three [that the primary objects of nature are to be
desired for virtue's sake, that virtue is to be desired for their sake, or
that virtue and these objects are to be desired each for their own
35 sake] is true and to be adopted he attempts to show in the following
manner. As it is the supreme good, not of a tree, or of a beast, or of a
god, but of man that philosophy is in quest of, he thinks that, first of
all, we must define man. He is of opinion that there are two parts in
human nature, body and soul, and makes no doubt that of these two
40 the soul is the better and by far the more worthy part. But whether
the soul alone is the man, so that the body holds the same relation
to it as a horse to the horseman, this he thinks has to be
ascertained. The horseman is not a horse and a man, but only a
man, yet he is called a horseman, because he is in some relation to
45 the horse. Again, is the body alone the man, having a relation to the
soul such as the cup has to the drink? For it is not the cup and the
drink it contains which are called the cup, but the cup alone; yet it is
so called because it is made to hold the drink. Or, lastly, is it neither
the soul alone nor the body alone, but both together, which are man,
50 the body and the soul being each a part, but the whole man being
both together, as we call two horses yoked together a pair, of which
pair the near and the off horse is each a part, but we do not call
either of them, no matter how connected with the other, a pair, but
only both together? Of these three alternatives, then, Varro chooses
55 the third, that man is neither the body alone, nor the soul alone, but
both together. And therefore the highest good, in which lies the
happiness of man, is composed of goods of both kinds, both bodily
and spiritual. And consequently he thinks that the primary objects of
nature are to be sought for their own sake, and that virtue, which is
60 the art of living, and can be communicated by instruction, is the most
excellent of spiritual goods. This virtue, then, or art of regulating life,
when it has received these primary objects of nature which existed
independently of it, and prior to any instruction, seeks them all, and
itself also, for its own sake; and it uses them, as it also uses itself,
65 that from them all it may derive profit and enjoyment, greater or
less, according as they are themselves greater or less; and while it

takes pleasure in all of them, it despises the less that it may obtain
or retain the greater when occasion demands. Now, of all goods,
spiritual or bodily, there is none at all to compare with virtue. For
70 virtue makes a good use both of itself and of all other goods in which
lies man's happiness; and where it is absent, no matter how many
good things a man has, they are not for his good, and consequently
should not be called good things while they belong to one who makes
them useless by using them badly. The life of man, then, is called
75 happy when it enjoys virtue and these other spiritual and bodily good
things without which virtue is impossible. It is called happier if it
enjoys some or many other good things which are not essential to
virtue; and happiest of all, if it lacks not one of the good things which
pertain to the body and the soul. For life is not the same thing as
80 virtue, since not every life, but a wisely regulated life, is virtue; and
yet, while there can be life of some kind without virtue, there cannot
be virtue without life. This I might apply to memory and reason, and
such mental faculties; for these exist prior to instruction, and without
them there cannot be any instruction, and consequently no virtue,
85 since virtue is learned. But bodily advantages, such as swiftness of
foot, beauty, or strength, are not essential to virtue, neither is virtue
essential to them, and yet they are good things; and, according to our
philosophers, even these advantages are desired by virtue for its own
sake, and are used and enjoyed by it in a becoming manner.
90 They say that this happy life is also social, and loves the
advantages of its friends as its own, and for their sake wishes for
them what it desires for itself, whether these friends live in the same
family, as a wife, children, domestics; or in the locality where one's
home is, as the citizens of the same town; or in the world at large, as
95 the nations bound in common human brotherhood; or in the universe
itself, comprehended in the heavens and the earth, as those whom
they call gods, and provide as friends for the wise man, and whom
we more familiarly call angels. Moreover, they say that, regarding the
supreme good and evil, there is no room for doubt, and that they
100 therefore differ from the New Academy in this respect, and they are
not concerned whether a philosopher pursues those ends which they
think true in the Cynic dress and manner of life or in some other.
And, lastly, in regard to the three modes of life, the contemplative,
the active, and the composite, they declare in favor of the third. That

105 these were the opinions and doctrines of the Old Academy, Varro
asserts on the authority of Antiochus, Cicero's master and his own,
though Cicero makes him out to have been more frequently in
accordance with the Stoics than with the Old Academy. But of what
importance is this to us, who ought to judge the matter on its own
110 merits, rather than to understand accurately what different men
have thought about it?

Chapter IV: What the Christians believe regarding the supreme
good and evil, in opposition to the philosophers, who have
maintained that the supreme good is in themselves.

115 If, then, we be asked what the city of God has to say upon these
points, and, in the first place, what its opinion regarding the
supreme good and evil is, it will reply that life eternal is the supreme
good, death eternal the supreme evil, and that to obtain the one and
escape the other we must live rightly. And thus it is written, "The
120 just lives by faith," for we do not as yet see our good, and must
therefore live by faith; neither have we in ourselves power to live
rightly, but can do so only if He who has given us faith to believe in
His help do help us when we believe and pray. As for those who have
supposed that the sovereign good and evil are to be found in this life,
125 and have placed it either in the soul or the body, or in both, or, to
speak more explicitly, either in pleasure or in virtue, or in both; in
repose or in virtue, or in both; in pleasure and repose, or in virtue, or
in all combined; in the primary objects of nature, or in virtue, or in
both—all these have, with a marvelous shallowness, sought to find
130 their blessedness in this life and in themselves. Contempt has been
poured upon such ideas by the Truth, saying by the prophet, "The
Lord knoweth the thoughts of men" (or, as the Apostle Paul cites the
passage, "The Lord knoweth the thoughts of the wise") "that they are
vain."

135 For what flood of eloquence can suffice to detail the miseries of
this life? Cicero, in the Consolation on the death of his daughter, has
spent all his ability in lamentation; but how inadequate was even
his ability here? For when, where, how, in this life can these primary
objects of nature be possessed so that they may not be assailed by
140 unforeseen accidents? Is the body of the wise man exempt from any
pain which may dispel pleasure, from any disquietude which may
banish repose? The amputation or decay of the members of the body

puts an end to its integrity, deformity blights its beauty, weakness
its health, lassitude its vigor, sleepiness or sluggishness its
145 activity—and which of these is it that may not assail the flesh of the
wise man? Comely and fitting attitudes and movements of the body
are numbered among the prime natural blessings; but what if some
sickness makes the members tremble? what if a man suffers from
curvature of the spine to such an extent that his hands reach the
150 ground, and he goes upon all fours like a quadruped? Does not this
destroy all beauty and grace in the body, whether at rest or in
motion? What shall I say of the fundamental blessings of the soul,
sense and intellect, of which the one is given for the perception, and
the other for the comprehension of truth? But what kind of sense is it
155 that remains when a man becomes deaf and blind? where are reason
and intellect when disease makes a man delirious? We can scarcely,
or not at all, refrain from tears, when we think of or see the actions
and words of such frantic persons, and consider how different from
and even opposed to their own sober judgment and ordinary conduct
160 their present demeanor is. And what shall I say of those who suffer
from demoniacal possession? Where is their own intelligence hidden
and buried while the malignant spirit is using their body and soul
according to his own will? And who is quite sure that no such thing
can happen to the wise man in this life?

165 Then, as to the perception of truth, what can we hope for even in
this way while in the body, as we read in the true book of Wisdom,
"The corruptible body weigheth down the soul, and the earthly
tabernacle presseth down the mind that museth upon many things?"
And eagerness, or desire of action, if this is the right meaning to put
170 upon the Greek oJrmhv, is also reckoned among the primary advantages
of nature; and yet is it not this which produces those pitiable
movements of the insane, and those actions which we shudder to see,
when sense is deceived and reason deranged?

In fine, virtue itself, which is not among the primary objects of
175 nature, but succeeds to them as the result of learning, though it
holds the highest place among human good things, what is its
occupation save to wage perpetual war with vices—not those that are
outside of us, but within; not other men's, but our own—a war which
is waged especially by that virtue which the Greeks call swfrsuvnh,
180 and we temperance, and which bridles carnal lusts, and prevents

them from winning the consent of the spirit to wicked deeds? For we must not fancy that there is no vice in us, when, as the apostle says, "The flesh lusteth against the spirit;" for to this vice there is a contrary virtue, when, as the same writer says, "The spirit lusteth
185 against the flesh." "For these two," he says, "are contrary one to the other, so that you cannot do the things which you would." But what is it we wish to do when we seek to attain the supreme good, unless that the flesh should cease to lust against the spirit, and that there be no vice in us against which the spirit may lust? And as we cannot
190 attain to this in the present life, however ardently we desire it, let us by God's help accomplish at least this, to preserve the soul from succumbing and yielding to the flesh that lusts against it, and to refuse our consent to the perpetration of sin. Far be it from us, then, to fancy that while we are still engaged in this intestine war, we
195 have already found the happiness which we seek to reach by victory. And who is there so wise that he has no conflict at all to maintain against his vices?

What shall I say of that virtue which is called prudence? Is not all its vigilance spent in the discernment of good from evil things, so
200 that no mistake may be admitted about what we should desire and what avoid? And thus it is itself a proof that we are in the midst of evils, or that evils are in us; for it teaches us that it is an evil to consent to sin, and a good to refuse this consent. And yet this evil, to which prudence teaches and temperance enables us not to consent, is
205 removed from this life neither by prudence nor by temperance. And justice, whose office it is to render to every man his due, whereby there is in man himself a certain just order of nature, so that the soul is subjected to God, and the flesh to the soul, and consequently both soul and flesh to God—does not this virtue demonstrate that it is as
210 yet rather laboring towards its end than resting in its finished work? For the soul is so much the less subjected to God as it is less occupied with the thought of God; and the flesh is so much the less subjected to the spirit as it lusts more vehemently against the spirit. So long, therefore, as we are beset by this weakness, this plague,
215 this disease, how shall we dare to say that we are safe? and if not safe, then how can we be already enjoying our final beatitude? Then that virtue which goes by the name of fortitude is the plainest proof of the ills of life, for it is these ills which it is compelled to bear

patiently. And this holds good, no matter though the ripest wisdom
co-exists with it. And I am at a loss to understand how the Stoic
philosophers can presume to say that these are no ills, though at the
same time they allow the wise man to commit suicide and pass out
of this life if they become so grievous that he cannot or ought not to
endure them. But such is the stupid pride of these men who fancy
that the supreme good can be found in this life, and that they can
become happy by their own resources, that their wise man, or at
least the man whom they fancifully depict as such, is always happy,
even though he become blind, deaf, dumb, mutilated, racked with
pains, or suffer any conceivable calamity such as may compel him to
make away with himself; and they are not ashamed to call the life
that is beset with these evils happy. O happy life, which seeks the
aid of death to end it? If it is happy, let the wise man remain in it;
but if these ills drive him out of it, in what sense is it happy? Or how
can they say that these are not evils which conquer the virtue of
fortitude, and force it not only to yield, but so to rave that it in one
breath calls life happy and recommends it to be given up? For who is
so blind as not to see that if it were happy it would not be fled from?
And if they say we should flee from it on account of the infirmities
that beset it, why then do they not lower their pride and
acknowledge that it is miserable?

Was it, I would ask, fortitude or weakness which prompted Cato
to kill himself? for he would not have done so had he not been too
weak to endure Caesar's victory. Where, then, is his fortitude? It has
yielded, it has succumbed, it has been so thoroughly overcome as to
abandon, forsake, flee this happy life. Or was it no longer happy?
Then it was miserable. How, then, were these not evils which made
life miserable, and a thing to be escaped from?

And therefore those who admit that these are evils, as the
Peripatetics do, and the Old Academy, the sect which Varro
advocates, express a more intelligible doctrine; but theirs also is a
surprising mistake, for they contend that this is a happy life which is
beset by these evils, even though they be so great that he who
endures them should commit suicide to escape them. "Pains and
anguish of body," says Varro, "are evils, and so much the worse in
proportion to their severity; and to escape them you must quit this
life." What life, I pray? This life, he says, which is oppressed by such

evils. Then it is happy in the midst of these very evils on account of
which you say we must quit it? Or do you call it happy because you
are at liberty to escape these evils by death? What, then, if by some
260   secret judgment of God you were held fast and not permitted to die,
nor suffered to live without these evils? In that case, at least, you
would say that such a life was miserable.

   It is soon relinquished, no doubt but this does not make it not
miserable; for were it eternal, you yourself would pronounce it
265   miserable. Its brevity, therefore, does not clear it of misery; neither
ought it to be called happiness because it is a brief misery. Certainly
there is a mighty force in these evils which compel a man—according
to them even a wise man—to cease to be a man that he may escape
them, though they say, and say truly, that it is as it were the first
270   and strongest demand of nature that a man cherish himself, and
naturally therefore avoid death, and should so stand his own friend
as to wish and vehemently aim at continuing to exist as a living
creature, and subsisting in this union of soul and body. There is a
mighty force in these evils to overcome this natural instinct by which
275   death is by every means and with all a man's efforts avoided, and to
overcome it so completely that what was avoided is desired, sought
after, and if it cannot in any other way be obtained, is inflicted by the
man on himself. There is a mighty force in these evils which make
fortitude a homicide—if, indeed, that is to be called fortitude which is
280   so thoroughly overcome by these evils, that it not only cannot
preserve by patience the man whom it undertook to govern and
defend, but is itself obliged to kill him. The wise man, I admit, ought
to bear death with patience, but when it is inflicted by another. If,
then, as these men maintain, he is obliged to inflict it on himself,
285   certainly it must be owned that the ills which compel him to this are
not only evils, but intolerable evils. The life, then, which is either
subject to accidents, or environed with evils so considerable and
grievous, could never have been called happy, if the men who give it
this name had condescended to yield to the truth, and to be
290   conquered by valid arguments, when they inquired after the happy
life, as they yield to unhappiness, and are overcome by overwhelming
evils, when they put themselves to death, and if they had not fancied
that the supreme good was to be found in this mortal life; for the very
virtues of this life, which are certainly its best and most useful

295 possessions, are all the more telling proofs of its miseries in
proportion as they are helpful against the violence of its dangers,
toils, and woes. For if these are true virtues—and such cannot exist
save in those who have true piety—they do not profess to be able to
deliver the men who possess them from all miseries; for true virtues
300 tell no such lies, but they profess that by the hope of the future world
this life, which is miserably involved in the many and great evils of
this world, is happy as it is also safe. For if not yet safe, how could it
be happy? And therefore the Apostle Paul, speaking not of men
without prudence, temperance, fortitude, and justice, but of those
305 whose lives were regulated by true piety, and whose virtues were
therefore true, says, "For we are saved by hope: now hope which is
seen is not hope; for what a man seeth, why doth he yet hope for?
But if we hope for that we see not, then do we with patience wait for
it." As, therefore, we are saved, so we are made happy by hope. And
310 as we do not as yet possess a present, but look for a future salvation,
so is it with our happiness, and this "with patience;" for we are
encompassed with evils, which we ought patiently to endure, until we
come to the ineffable enjoyment of unmixed good; for there shall be no
longer anything to endure. Salvation, such as it shall be in the world
315 to come, shall itself be our final happiness. And this happiness these
philosophers refuse to believe in, because they do not see it, and
attempt to fabricate for themselves a happiness in this life, based
upon a virtue which is as deceitful as it is proud.

Boethius: The Consolation of Philosophy

Imprisoned and awaiting execution, Boethius (480-524) engages in dialogue with Lady Philosophy, who represents Reason. Philosophy successfully persuades the despairing Boethius not to place his trust in false images of human happiness, which are now beyond his grasp, but in the genuine and ultimate human good, which is not absent from him even in his prison cell.

In the work as written, Boethius alternated the prose passages given below with poetic verses, which we have omitted.

BOOK III

Prose 1

When she finished her song, its soothing tones left me spellbound with my ears alert in my eagerness to listen. So a while afterwards I said, Greatest comforter of weary minds, how have you cheered me with your deep thoughts and sweet singing too! No more shall I
5   doubt my power to meet the blows of Fortune. So far am I from terror at the remedies which you did lately tell me were sharper, that I am longing to hear them, and eagerly I beg you for them.

Then said she, I knew it when you laid hold upon my words in silent attention, and I was waiting for that frame of mind in you, or
10   more truly, I brought it about in you. They that remain are indeed bitter to the tongue, but sweet to the inner man. But as you say you are eager to hear, how ardently you would be burning, if you knew where I am attempting to lead you!

Where is that? I asked.

15   To the true happiness, of which your soul too dreams; but your sight is taken up in imaginary views thereof, so that you cannot look upon itself.

Then said I, I pray you show me what that truly is, and quickly.

I will do so, she said, willingly for your sake. But first I will try to
20   picture in words and give you the form of the cause, which is already better known to you, so that, when that picture is perfect and you

53

turn your eyes to the other side, you may recognize the form of true
happiness.

Prose 2

She lowered her eyes for a little while as though searching the
innermost recesses of her mind; and then she continued: The trouble
of the many and various aims of mortal men bring them much care,
and herein they go forward by different paths but strive to reach one
end, which is happiness. And that good is that, to which if any man
attain, he can desire nothing further. It is that highest of all good
things, and it embraces in itself all good things: if any good is
lacking, it cannot be the highest good, since then there is left outside
it something which can be desired. Wherefore happiness is a state
which is made perfect by the union of all good things. This end all
men seek to reach, as I said, though by different paths. For there is
implanted by nature in the minds of men a desire for the true good;
but error leads them astray towards false goods by wrong paths.

Some men believe that the highest good is to lack nothing, and so
they are at pains to possess abundant riches. Others consider the
true good to be that which is most worthy of admiration, and so they
strive to attain to places of honor, and to be held by their fellow-
citizens in honor thereby. Some determine that the highest good lies
in the highest power; and so they either desire to reign themselves, or
try to cleave to those who do reign. Others think that renown is the
greatest good, and they therefore hasten to make a famous name by
the arts of peace or of war. But more than all measure the fruit of
good by pleasure and enjoyment, and these think that the happiest
man is abandoned to pleasure. Further, there are those who confuse
the aims and the causes of these good things: as those who desire
riches for the sake of power or of pleasure, or those who seek power
for the sake of money or celebrity.

In these, then, and other things like to them, lies the aim of
men's actions and prayers, such as renown and popularity, which
seem to afford some fame, or wife and children, which are sought for
the pleasure they give. On the other hand, the good of friends, which
is the most honorable and holy of all, lies not in Fortune's but in

Virtue's realm. All others are adopted for the sake of power or enjoyment.

Again, it is plain that the good things of the body must be accounted to those false causes which we have mentioned; for bodily strength and stature seem to make men more able and strong; beauty and swiftness seem to give renown; health seems to give pleasure. By all these happiness alone is plainly desired. For each man holds that to be the highest good, which he seeks before all others. But we have defined the highest good to be happiness. Wherefore what each man desires above all others, he holds to be a state of happiness.

Wherefore you have each of these placed before you as the form of human happiness: wealth, honors, power, glory, and pleasure. Epicurus considered these forms alone, and accordingly determined upon pleasure as the highest good, because all the others seemed but to join with it in bringing enjoyment to the mind.

But to return to the aims of men: their minds seem to seek to regain the highest good, and their memories seem to dull their powers. It is as though a drunken man were seeking his home, but could not remember the way there. Can those people be altogether wrong whose aim it is to lack nothing? No, there is nothing which can make happiness so perfect as an abundant possession of good things, needing nothing that belongs to others, but in all ways sufficing for itself. Surely those others too are not mistaken who think that what is best is also most worthy of reverence and respect. It cannot be any cheap or base thing, to attain which almost all men aim and strive. And is power not to be accounted a good thing? Surely it is: can that be a weak thing or without force, which is allowed in all cases to excel? Is renown of no value? We cannot surrender this; that whatever is most excellent, has also great renown. It is hardly worth saying that happiness has no torturing cares or gloom, and is not subject to grief and trouble; for even in small things, the aim is to find that which it is a delight to have and to enjoy.

These, then, are the desires of men: they long for riches, places of honor, kingdoms, glory, and pleasure; and they long for them because they think that thereby they will find satisfaction, veneration, power, renown, and happiness. It is the good then which men seek by their different desires; and it is easy to show how great a force nature has

put therein, since in spite of such varying and discordant opinions,
95   they are all agreed in the goal they seek, that of the highest good.

Prose 3

And you too, creatures of the earth, do dream of your first state,
though with a dim idea. With whatsoever thinking it may be, you
look to that goal of happiness, though never so obscure your
thoughts: thither, to true happiness, your natural course does guide
100   you, and from the same your various errors lead you. For I would
have you consider whether men can reach the end they have resolved
upon, namely happiness, by these ways by which they think to
attain thereto. If money and places of honor and such-like do bring
anything of that sort to a man who seems to lack no good thing, then
105   let us acknowledge with them that men do become happy by the
possession of these things. But if they cannot perform their promises,
and there is still lack of further good things, surely it is plain that a
false appearance of happiness is there discovered. You, therefore,
who had lately abundant riches, shall first answer me. With all that
110   great wealth, was your mind never perturbed by torturing care
arising from some sense of injustice?
    Yes, I said; I cannot remember that my mind was ever free from
some such care.
    Was it not because something was lacking, which you missed, or
115   because something was present to you which you did not like to
have?
    Yes, I answered.
    You desired, then, the presence of the one, and the absence of the
other?
120   I acknowledge it.
    Then, said she, such a man lacks what he desires.
    He does.
    But while a man lacks anything, can he possibly satisfy himself?
    No, said I.
125   Then, while you were bountifully supplied with wealth, you felt
that you did not satisfy yourself?
    I did indeed.

Then, said she, wealth cannot prevent a man from lacking or make him satisfied. And this is what it apparently professed to do.

130 And this point too I feel is most important: money has in itself, by its own nature, nothing which can prevent its being carried off from those, who possess it, against their will.

It has not, I said.

No, you cannot deny that any stronger man may any day snatch

135 it from them. For how come about the quarrels of the law-courts ? Is it not because people try to regain money that has been by force or by fraud taken from them?

Yes, I answered.

Then, said she, a man will need to seek from the outside help to

140 guard his own money.

That cannot be denied, I said.

And a man will not need that unless he possesses money which he can lose.

Undoubtedly he will not.

145 Then the argument turns round the other way, she said. The riches which were thought to make a man all-sufficient for himself, do really put him in need of other people's help. Then how can need be separated from wealth? Do the rich never feel hunger nor thirst? Do the limbs of moneyed men never feel the cold of winter? You will say,

150 'Yes, but the rich have the wherewithal to satisfy hunger and thirst, and drive away cold.' But though riches may thus console wants, they cannot entirely take them away. For, though these ever crying wants, these continual requests, are satisfied, yet there must exist that which is to be satisfied. I need not say that nature is satisfied with

155 little, greed is never satisfied. Wherefore, I ask you, if wealth cannot remove want, and even creates its own wants, what reason is there that you should think it affords satisfaction to a man?

Prose 4

But, I urged, places of honor make the man, to whom they fall, honored and venerated.

160 Ah! she answered, have those offices their force in truth that they may instill virtues into the minds of those that hold them, and drive out vices therefrom? And yet we are too well accustomed to see them

making wickedness conspicuous rather than avoiding it. Wherefore
we are displeased to see such places often falling to the most wicked
165   of men, so that Catullus called Nonius 'a diseased growth', though he
sat in the highest chair of office. Do you see how great a disgrace high
honors can add to evil men? Their unworthiness is less conspicuous if
they are not made famous by honors. Could you yourself have been
induced by any dangers to think of being a colleague with Decoratus,
170   when you saw that he had the mind of an unscrupulous buffoon, and
a base informer? We cannot consider men worthy of veneration on
account of their high places, when we hold them to be unworthy of
those high places. But if you see a man endowed with wisdom, you
cannot but consider him worthy of veneration, or at least of the
175   wisdom with which he is endowed. For such a man has the worth
peculiar to virtue, which it transmits directly to those in whom it is
found. But since honors from the vulgar crowd cannot create merit, it
is plain that they have not the peculiar beauty of this worth. And
here is a particular point to be noticed: if men are the more worthless
180   as they are despised by more people, high position makes them all
the worse because it cannot make venerable those whom it shows to
so many people to be contemptible. And this brings its penalty with
it: wicked people bring a like quality into their positions, and stain
them with their infection.

185   Now I would have you consider the matter thus, that you may
recognize that true veneration cannot be won through these shadowy
honors. If a man who had filled the office of consul many times in
Rome, came by chance into a country of barbarians, would his high
position make him venerated by the barbarians? Yet if this were a
190   natural quality in such dignities, they would never lose their effective
function in any land, just as fire is never anything but hot in all
countries. But since they do not receive this quality of veneration from
any force peculiar to themselves, but only from a connection in the
untrustworthy opinions of men, they become as nothing as soon as
195   they are among those who do not consider these dignities as such.

But that is only in the case of foreign peoples. Among the very
peoples where they had their beginnings, do these dignities last for
ever? Consider how great was the power in Rome of old of the office of
Prefect: now it is an empty name and a heavy burden upon the
200   income of any man of Senator's rank. The prefect then, who was

commissioner of the corn-market, was held to be a great man. Now there is no office more despised. For, as I said before, that which has no intrinsic beauty, sometimes receives a certain glory, sometimes loses it, according to the opinion of those who are concerned with it. If
205 then high offices cannot make men venerated, if furthermore they grow vile by the infection of bad men, if changes of time can end their glory, and, lastly, if they are held cheaply in the estimation of whole peoples, I ask you, so far from affording true beauty to men, what beauty have they in themselves which men can desire?

Prose 5

210 Can kingdoms and intimacies with kings make people powerful? 'Certainly,' some may answer, 'in so far as their happiness is lasting.' But antiquity and our times too are full of examples of the contrary; examples of men whose happiness as kings has been exchanged for disaster. What wonderful power, which is found to be powerless even
215 for its own preservation! But if this kingly power is really a source of happiness, surely then, if it fail in any way, it lessens the happiness it brings, and equally causes unhappiness. However widely human empires may extend, there must be still more nations left, over whom each king does not reign. And so, in whatever direction this power
220 ceases to make happy, thereby comes in powerlessness, which makes men unhappy; thus therefore there must be a greater part of unhappiness in every king's estate. That tyrant had learned well the dangers of his lot, who likened the fear which goes with kingship to the terror inspired by a sword ever hanging overhead.
225 What then is such a power, which cannot drive away the bite of cares, nor escape the stings of fear? Yet these all would willingly live without fear, but they cannot, and yet they boast of their power. Think you a man is powerful when you see that he longs for that which he cannot bring to pass? Do you reckon a man powerful who
230 walks abroad with dignity and attended by servants? A man who strikes fear into his subjects, yet fears them more himself? A man who must be at the mercy of those that serve him, in order that he may seem to have power?
Need I speak of intimacies with kings when kingship itself is
235 shown to be full of weakness? Not only when kings' powers fall are

their friends laid low, but often even when their powers are intact.
Nero compelled his friend and tutor, Seneca, to choose how he would
die. Papinianus, for a long while a powerful courtier, was handed
over to the soldiers' swords by the Emperor Antoninus. Yet each of
240   these was willing to surrender all his power. Seneca even tried to give
up all his wealth to Nero, and to seek retirement. But the very
weight of their wealth and power dragged them down to ruin, and
neither could do what he wished.

What then is that power, whose possessors fear it? in desiring to
245   possess which, you are not safe, and from which you cannot escape,
even though you try to lay it down? What help are friends, made not
by virtue but by fortune? The friend gained by good fortune becomes
an enemy in ill-fortune. And what plague can more effectively injure
than an intimate enemy?

Prose 6

250   How deceitful is fame often, and how base a thing it is! Justly did
the tragic poet cry out, 'O Fame, Fame, how many lives of little men
have you puffed up!' For many men have got a great name from the
false opinions of the crowd. And what could be baser than such a
thing? For those who are falsely praised, must blush to hear their
255   praises. And if they are justly won by merits, what can they add to
the pleasure of a wise man's conscience? For he measures his
happiness not by popular talk, but by the truth of his conscience. If it
attracts a man to make his name widely known, he must equally
think it a shame if it be not made known. But I have already said
260   that there must be yet more lands into which the renown of a single
man can never come; wherefore it follows that the man, whom you
think famous, will seem to have no such fame in the next quarter of
the earth.

Popular favor seems to me to be unworthy even of mention under
265   this head, for it comes not by any judgment, and is never constant.
Again, who can but see how empty a name, and how futile, is noble
birth? For if its glory is due to renown, it belongs not to the man. For
the glory of noble birth seems to be praise for the merits of a man's
forefathers. But if praise creates the renown, it is the renowned who
270   are praised. Wherefore, if you have no renown of your own, that of

others cannot glorify you. But if there is any good in noble birth, I conceive it to be this, and this alone, that the highborn seem to be bound in honor not to show any degeneracy from their fathers' virtue.

Prose 7

And now what am I to say of the pleasures of the body? The desires of the flesh are full of cares, their fulfillment is full of remorse. What terrible diseases, what unbearable griefs, truly the fruits of sin, do they bring upon the bodies of those who enjoy them! I know not what pleasure their impulse affords, but any who cares to recall his indulgences of his passions, will know that the results of such pleasures are indeed gloomy. If any can show that those results are blessed with happiness, then may the beasts of the field be justly called blessed, for all their aims are urged toward the satisfying of their bodies' wants. The pleasures of wife and children may be most honorable; but nature makes it all too plain that some have found torment in their children. How bitter is any such kind of suffering, I need not tell you now, for you have never known it, nor have any such anxiety now. Yet in this matter I would hold with my philosopher Euripides, that he who has no children is happy in his misfortune.

Prose 8

There is then no doubt that these roads to happiness are no roads, and they cannot lead any man to any end whither they profess to take him. I would show you shortly with what great evils they are bound up.

Would you heap up money? You will need to tear it from its owner. Would you seem brilliant by the glory of great honors? You must kneel before their dispenser, and in your desire to surpass other men in honor, you must debase yourself by setting aside all pride. Do you long for power? You will be subject to the wiles of all over whom you have power, you will be at the mercy of many dangers. You seek fame? You will be drawn to and fro among rough paths, and lose all freedom from care. Would you spend a life of pleasure? Who would not despise and cast off such servitude to so vile and brittle a thing as your body? How petty are all the aims of those who put before themselves the pleasures of the body, how uncertain is the possession of such? In bodily size will you ever surpass the elephant? In strength will you ever lead the bull, or in speed the tiger?

Look upon the expanse of heaven, the strength with which it stands, the rapidity with which it moves, and cease for a while to wonder at base things. This heaven is not more wonderful for those things than for the design which guides it. How sweeping is the brightness of outward form, how swift its movement, yet more fleeting than the passing of the flowers of spring. But if, as Aristotle says, many could use the eyes of Lynceus to see through that which meets the eye, then if they saw into the organs within, would not that body, though it had the most fair outside of Alcibiades, seem most vile within? Wherefore it is not your own nature, but the weakness of the eyes of them that see you, which makes you seem beautiful. But consider how in excess you desire the pleasures of the body, when you know that howsoever you admire it, it can be reduced to nothing by a three-day fever.

To put all these points then in a word: these things cannot grant the good which they promise; they are not made perfect by the union of all good things in them; they do not lead to happiness as a path there; they do not make men blessed.

Prose 9

So far, she continued, we have been content to set forth the form of false happiness. If you clearly understand that, my next duty is to show what is true happiness.

I do see, said I, that wealth cannot satisfy, that power comes not to kingdoms, nor veneration to high offices; that true renown cannot accompany ambition, nor true enjoyment wait upon the pleasures of the body.

Have you grasped the reasons why it is so? she asked.

I seem to look at them as through a narrow chink, but I would learn more clearly from you.

The reason is to hand, said she; human error takes that which is simple and by nature impossible to divide, tries to divide it, and turns its truth and perfection into falsity and imperfection. Tell me, do you think that anything which lacks nothing, can be without power?

340   Of course not.

You are right; for if anything has any weakness in any part, it must lack the help of something else.

That is so, I said.

Then perfect satisfaction and power have the same nature?

345   Yes, it seems so.

And do you think such a thing contemptible, or the opposite, worthy of all veneration?

There can be no doubt that it is worthy.

Then let us add veneration to that satisfaction and power, and

350   so consider these three as one.

Yes, we must add it if we wish to proclaim the truth.

Do you then think that this whole is dull and of no reputation, or renowned with all glory? For consider it thus: we have granted that it lacks nothing, that it has all power and is worthy of all veneration; it

355   must not therefore lack the glory which it cannot supply for itself, and thereby seem to be in any direction contemptible.

No, I said, I must allow that it has glory too.

Therefore we must rank this glory equally with the other three.

Yes, we must.

360   Then that which lacks nothing from outside itself, which is all-powerful by its own might, which has renown and veneration, must surely be allowed to be most happy too?

I cannot imagine from what quarter unhappiness would creep into such a thing, wherefore we must grant that it is full of happiness

365   if the other qualities remain existent.

Then it follows further, that though perfect satisfaction, power, glory, veneration, and happiness differ in name, they cannot differ at all in essence?

They cannot.

370   This then, said she, is a simple, single thing by nature, only divided by the mistakes of base humanity; and while men try to gain a part of that which has no parts, they fail both to obtain a fraction, which cannot exist, and the whole too after which they do not strive.

Tell me how they fail thus, I said.

375   One seeks riches by fleeing from poverty, and takes no thought of power,' she answered, 'and so he prefers to be base and unknown, and even deprives himself of natural pleasures lest he should part with the riches which he has gathered. Thus not even that satisfaction reaches the man who loses all power, who is stabbed by

380 sorrow, lowered by his meanness, hidden by his lack of fame. Another seeks power only: he scatters his wealth, he despises pleasures and honors which have no power, and sets no value upon glory. You see how many things such an one lacks. Sometimes he goes without necessaries even, sometimes he feels the bite and

385 torture of care; and as he cannot rid himself of these, he loses the power too which he sought above all things. The same argument may be applied to offices, glory, and pleasure. For since each one of these is the same as each other, any man who seeks one without the others, gains not even that one which he desires.

390   What then? I asked.

    If any man desires to obtain all together, he will be seeking the sum of happiness. But will he ever find that in these things which we have shown cannot supply what they promise?

    No.

395   Then happiness is not to be sought for among these things which are separately believed to supply each thing so sought.

    Nothing could be more plainly true, I said.

    Then you have before you the form of false happiness, and its causes; now turn your attention in the opposite direction, and you

400 will quickly see the true happiness which I have promised to show you.

    But surely this is clear even to the blindest, and you showed it before when you were trying to make clear the causes of false happiness. For if I mistake not, true and perfect happiness is that

405 which makes a man truly satisfied, powerful, venerated, renowned, and happy. And (for I would have you see that I have looked deeply into the matter) I realize without doubt that that which can truly yield any one of these, since they are all one, is perfect happiness.

    Ah! my son, said she, I do see that you are blessed in this

410 opinion, but I would have you add one thing.

    What is that? I asked.

Do you think that there is anything among mortals, and in our perishable lives, which could yield such a state?

I do not think that there is, and I think that you have shown this
415   beyond the need of further proof.

These then seem to yield to mortals certain appearances of the true good, or some such imperfections; but they cannot give true and perfect good.

No.

420   Since, then, you have seen what is true happiness, and what are the false imitations of it, it now remains that you should learn where this true happiness may be sought.

For that, said I, I have been impatiently waiting.

But divine help must be sought in small things as well as great
425   (as my pupil Plato says in his Timaeus); so what, think you, must we do to deserve to find the place of that highest good?

Call, I said, upon the Father of all, for if we do not do so, no undertaking would be rightly or duly begun.

'You are right,' said she...

Prose 10

430   Since then you have seen the form both of the imperfect and the perfect good, I think I should now show you where lies this perfection of happiness. In this I think our first inquiry must be whether any good of this kind can exist in the very nature of a subject; for we must not let any vain form of thought make us miss the truth of this
435   matter. But there can be no denial of its existence, that it is as the very source of all good. For if anything is said to be imperfect, it is held to be so by some loss of its perfection. Wherefore if in any kind of thing a particular seems imperfect, there must also be a perfect specimen in the same kind. For if you take away the perfection, it is
440   impossible even to imagine whence could come the so-called imperfect specimen. For nature does not start from degenerate or imperfect specimens, but starting from the perfect and ideal, it degenerates to these lower and weaker forms.

If then, as we have shown above, there is an uncertain and
445   imperfect happiness to be found in the good, then there must doubtless be also a sure and perfect happiness therein.

Yes, said I, that is quite surely proved to be true.

Now consider, she continued, where it lies. The universally accepted notion of men proves that God, the fountain-head of all
450   things, is good. For nothing can be thought of better than God, and surely He, than whom there is nothing better, must without doubt be good. Now reason shows us that God is so good, that we are convinced that in Him lies also the perfect good. For if it is not so, He cannot be the fountain-head; for there must then be something more
455   excellent, possessing that perfect good, which appears to be of older origin than God: for it has been proved that all perfections are of earlier origin than the imperfect specimens of the same: wherefore, unless we are to prolong the series to infinity, we must allow that the highest Deity must be full of the highest, the perfect good. But as we
460   have laid down that true happiness is perfect good, it must be that true happiness is situated in His Divinity.

Yes, I accept that; it cannot be in any way contradicted.

But, she said, I beg you, be sure that you accept with a sure conscience and determination this fact, that we have said that the
465   highest Deity is filled with the highest good.

How should I think of it? I asked.

You must not think of God, the Father of all, whom we hold to be filled with the highest good, as having received this good into Himself from without, nor that He has it by nature in such a manner that you
470   might consider Him, its possessor, and the happiness possessed, as having different essential existences. For if you think that good has been received from without, that which gave it must be more excellent than that which received it; but we have most rightly stated that He is the most excellent of all things. And if you think that it is
475   in Him by His nature, but different in kind, then, while we speak of God as the fountain-head of all things, who could imagine by whom these different kinds can have been united? Lastly, that which is different from anything cannot be the thing from which it differs. So anything which is by its nature different from the highest good,
480   cannot be the highest good. And this we must not think of God, than whom there is nothing more excellent, as we have agreed. Nothing in this world can have a nature which is better than its origin, wherefore I would conclude that that which is the origin of all things, according to the truest reasoning, is by its essence the highest good.

485 Most truly, I said.

You agree that the highest good is happiness?

Yes.

Then you must allow that God is absolute happiness?

I cannot deny what you put forward before, and I see that this

490 follows necessarily from those propositions.

Look then, she said, whether it is proved more strongly by this too: there cannot be two highest goods which are different. For where two good things are different, the one cannot be the other; wherefore neither can be the perfect good, while each is lacking to the other.

495 And that which is not perfect cannot be the highest, plainly. Therefore if two things are highest good, they cannot be different. Further, we have proved to ourselves that both happiness and God are each the highest good. Therefore the highest Deity must be identical with the highest happiness.

500 No conclusion, I said, could be truer in fact, or more surely proved by reason, or more worthy of our God.

Besides this let me give you corollary, as geometricians do, when they wish to add a point drawn from the propositions they have proved. Since men become happy by acquiring happiness, and

505 happiness is identical with divinity, it is plain that they become happy by acquiring divinity. But just as men become just by acquiring the quality of justice, and wise by wisdom, so by the same reasoning, by acquiring divinity they become divine. Every happy man then is divine. But while nothing prevents as many men as

510 possible from being divine, God is so by His nature, men become so by participation.

This corollary, I said, or whatever you call it, is indeed beautiful and very precious.

Yes, but nothing can be more beautiful than this too which

515 reason would have us add to what we have agreed upon.

What is that? I asked.

Happiness seems to include many things: do all these join it together as into a whole which is happiness, as though each thing were a different part thereof, or is any one of them a good which

520 fulfills the essence of happiness, and do the others merely bear relations to this one?

I would have you make this plain by the enunciation of these particulars.

Do we not, she asked, hold that happiness is a good thing?

525 Yes, I answered, the highest good.

But you may apply this quality of happiness to them all. For the perfect satisfaction is the same, and the highest power, and veneration, and renown, and pleasure; these are all held to be happiness.

530 What then? I asked.

Are all these things, satisfaction, power, and the others, as it were, members of the body, happiness, or do they all bear their relation to the good, as members to a head?

I understand what you propose to examine, but I am waiting 535 eagerly to hear what you will lay down.

I would have you take the following explanation, she said. If these were all members of the one body, happiness, they would differ individually. For this is the nature of particulars, to make up one body of different parts. But all these have been shown to be one and 540 the same. Therefore they are not as members; and further, this happiness will then appear to be joined together into a whole body out of one member, which is impossible.

That is quite certain, said I, but I would hear what is to come.

It is plain that the others have some relation to the good. It is for 545 that reason, namely because it is held to be good, that this satisfaction is sought, and power likewise, and the others too; we may suppose the same of veneration, renown, and pleasure. The good then is the cause of the desire for all of these, and their consummation also. Such a thing as has in itself no real or even 550 pretended good, cannot ever be sought. On the other hand, such things as are not by nature good, but seem to be so, are sought as though they were truly good. Wherefore we may justly believe that their good quality is the cause of the desire for them, the very hinge on which they turn, and their consummation. The really important 555 object of a desire, is that for the sake of which anything is sought, as a means. For instance, if a man wishes to ride for the sake of his health, he does not so much desire the motion of riding, as the effect, namely health. As, therefore, each of these things is desired for the sake of the good, the absolute good is the aim, rather than

560 themselves. But we have agreed that the other things are desired for the sake of happiness, wherefore in this case too, it is happiness alone which is the object of the desire. Wherefore it is plain that the essence of the good and of happiness is one and the same.

I cannot see how any one can think otherwise.

565 But we have shown that God and true happiness are one and the same.

Yes.

Therefore, said she, we may safely conclude that the essence of God also lies in the absolute good and nowhere else.

St. Thomas Aquinas, *Treatise on Law*

QUESTION NINETY

OF THE ESSENCE OF LAW

Article 1: Whether law is something belonging to reason?

Law is a certain rule and measure of actions, whereby one is induced to act or is restrained from acting: for <u>lex</u> [law] is derived from <u>ligando</u> [to bind], since it binds one to act. Now the rule and measure of human acts is the reason, which is the first principle of
5   human acts, as is clear from what has been said above: for it belongs to the reason to order [things] to an end, which is the first principle in all matters of action, according to the Philosopher. Now that which is the principle in any genus is the rule and measure of that genus: as unity in the genus of number and the first motion in the genus of
10   motions. Consequently it follows that law is something pertaining to reason.

Article 2: Whether law is always ordered to the common good?

As was said, the law pertains to that which is a principle of human acts, since it is a rule and measure. Now as reason is a
15   principle of human acts, so in reason itself there is something which is the principle in respect of all the rest: wherefore law pertains chiefly and mainly to this principle. Now the first principle in practical matters, which are the object of the practical reason, is the final end: and the final end of human life is happiness or
20   blessedness, as stated above. Consequently the law must regard principally the ordering [of means] to happiness.

Moreover, since every part is ordered to the whole, as imperfect to perfect; and since one man is a part of the perfect community, the law must properly regard the ordering [of means] to common
25   happiness. Wherefore the Philosopher, in the above definition of legal matters, mentions both happiness and the body politic: for he says that "we call those legal matters 'just' which are adapted to produce

71

and preserve happiness and its parts for the body politic": for the state is a perfect community, as he says in the <u>Politics</u>, I, 1.

30 Now in every genus, that which belongs to it chiefly is the principle of the others, and the others belong to that genus in subordination to that thing: thus fire, which is chief among hot things, is the cause of heat in mixed bodies, and these are said to be hot in so far as they have a share of fire. Consequently, since the law

35 is chiefly ordained to the common good, any other precept in regard to some individual work, must be devoid of the nature of a law, save in so far as it regards the common good. Therefore every law is ordered to the common good.

Article 3: Whether the reason of just any man is able to make a law?

40 A law, properly speaking, regards first and foremost an ordering to the common good. Now to order anything to the common good, pertains either to the whole people, or to someone who is the viceregent of the whole people. And therefore the framing of a law pertains either to the whole people or to a public personage who has

45 care of the whole people: since in all other matters the ordering of anything to an end belongs to him to whom the end belongs.

Article 4: Whether promulgation is essential to a law?

As was said, a law is imposed on others as a rule and measure. Now a rule or measure is imposed in being applied to those who are to be ruled and measured by it. Wherefore, in order that a law obtain

50 the binding force which is proper to a law, it must be applied to those who are to be ruled by it. Such application is made in its being made known to them by promulgation. Wherefore promulgation is necessary for the law to obtain its force.

Thus from the four preceding articles, the definition of law may

55 be gathered: and it is nothing else than an ordering of reason for the common good, by him who has care of the community, and promulgated.

QUESTION NINETY-ONE

OF THE VARIOUS KINDS OF LAW

Article 2: Whether there is a natural law in us?

Objection 3: The more a man is free, the less is he under the law. But man is freer than all the animals, on account of his free will, which he has above all other animals. Since therefore other animals are not subject to a natural law, neither is man subject to a natural law.

On the contrary, A gloss on Rm 2:14: "When the Gentiles, who have not the law, do by nature those things that are of the law," says: "Although they have no written law, yet they have the natural law, whereby each one knows, and is conscious of, what is good and what is evil."

As was said above, law, since it is a rule and measure, can be in someone in two ways: in one way, as in him that rules and measures; in another way, as in that which is ruled and measured, since a thing is ruled and measured insofar as it partakes of the rule or measure. Wherefore, since all things subject to Divine providence are ruled and measured by the eternal law, as is clear from what has been said; it is manifest that all things partake somewhat of the eternal law, insofar as they derive their respective inclinations to their proper acts and ends from its being imprinted on them. Now among all others, the rational creature is subject to Divine providence in the most excellent way, insofar as it partakes of a share of providence, by being provident both for itself and for others. Wherefore it has a share of the Eternal Reason, whereby it has a natural inclination to its proper act and end: and this participation of the eternal law in the rational creature is called the natural law. Hence the Psalmist after saying (Ps 4:6): "Offer up the sacrifice of justice," as though someone asked what the works of justice are, adds: "Many say, Who showeth us good things?" in answer to which question he says: "The light of Thy countenance, O Lord, is signed upon us": thus implying that the light of natural reason, whereby we discern what is good and what is evil, which is the function of the natural law, is nothing else than an imprint on us of the Divine light.

90   It is therefore evident that the natural law is nothing else than the
rational creature's participation of the eternal law.

Reply To Objection 3: Even irrational animals partake in their
own way of the Eternal Reason, just as the rational creature does.
But because the rational creature partakes of it in an intellectual
95   and rational manner, therefore the participation of the eternal law in
the rational creature is properly called a law, since a law is
something pertaining to reason, as was said above (90, 1). Irrational
creatures, however, do not partake of it in a rational manner,
wherefore it cannot be called a law except by way of similitude.

Article 3: Whether there is a human law?

100   As was said above, question 90, 1, <u>ad</u> 2, a law is a dictate of the
practical reason. Now it is to be observed that the same procedure is
found in the practical and in the speculative reason: for each proceeds
from principles to conclusions, as stated above (ibid.). Accordingly we
must say that just as, in the speculative reason, from naturally
105   known indemonstrable principles we draw the conclusions of the
various sciences, the knowledge of which is not imparted to us by
nature, but acquired by the efforts of reason, so too it is from the
precepts of the natural law, as from general and indemonstrable
principles, that the human reason needs to proceed to the more
110   particular determination of certain matters. These particular
determinations, discovered by human reason, are called human laws,
provided the other essential conditions of law, as were noted above
(90, 2-4) are observed. Wherefore Tully [Cicero] says in his <u>Rhetoric</u>
(2, 53) that "justice has its source in nature; thence certain things
115   came into custom by reason of their utility; afterwards these things
which emanated from nature and were approved by custom, were
sanctioned by fear and reverence for the law."

QUESTION NINETY-FOUR

OF THE NATURAL LAW

Article 2: Whether the natural law contains many precepts, or only one?

As stated above (91, 3), the precepts of the natural law are to the practical reason what the first principles of demonstration are to the speculative reason: for both are self-evident principles. Now a thing is said to be self-evident in two ways: first, in itself; secondly, in relation to us. Any proposition is said to be self-evident in itself if its predicate is contained in the notion of the subject: although, to one who does not know the definition of the subject, it happens that such a proposition is not self-evident.

For instance, this proposition, 'man is rational,' is in its very nature self-evident, since whoever says 'man' says 'rational': and yet to one who knows not what a man is, this proposition is not self-evident. Hence it is that, as Boethius says (<u>De Hebdom</u>.), certain axioms or propositions are universally self-evident to all; and such are those propositions whose terms are known to all, as, 'every whole is greater than its part' and 'things equal to one and the same thing are equal to one another.'

But some propositions are self-evident only to the wise, who understand the meaning of the terms of such propositions: thus to one who understands that an angel is not a body, it is self-evident that an angel is not circumscriptively in a place: but this is not evident to the unlearned, who do not grasp this.

Now a certain order is to be found in those things that are apprehended by all. For that which first falls under our apprehension is 'being,' the notion of which is included in all things whatsoever someone apprehends. Wherefore the first indemonstrable principle is that 'the same thing cannot be affirmed and denied at the same time,' which is based on the notion of 'being' and 'non-being': and on this principle all others are based, as is stated in the <u>Metaphysics</u> (IV, 3). Now as 'being' is the first thing that falls under the apprehension simply, so 'good' is the first thing that falls under the apprehension of the practical reason, which is directed to action:

150

155

since every agent acts for an end under the aspect of good. Consequently the first principle of practical reason is one founded on the notion of good, that is, 'the good is that which all things desire.' Consequently, this is the first precept of law, that 'good is to be done and pursued, and evil is to be avoided.' And all the other precepts of the natural law are based upon this: so that whatever the practical reason naturally apprehends as human goods (or evils) belongs to the precepts of the natural law as something to be done or avoided.

160

165

170

175

180

Since, however, good has the nature of an end, and evil, the nature of a contrary, hence it is that all those things to which man has a natural inclination are naturally apprehended by reason as being good, and consequently as objects of pursuit, and their contraries as evil, and objects of avoidance. Wherefore the order of the precepts of the natural law follows the order of our natural inclinations. Because in man there is first of all an inclination to good in accordance with the nature which he has in common with all substances: inasmuch as every substance seeks the preservation of its own being according to its nature: by reason of this inclination those things through which human life is preserved, and its obstacles are warded off, belong to the natural law. Secondly, there is in man an inclination to things that pertain to him more specially, according to that nature which he has in common with other animals: and in virtue of this inclination, those things are said to belong to the natural law, "which nature has taught to all animals," such as sexual intercourse, education of the young, and the like. Thirdly, there is in man an inclination to good, according to the nature of reason, which is proper to him: thus man has a natural inclination to know the truth about God, and to live in society: and in this respect, whatever pertains to this inclination belongs to the natural law; for instance, to avoid ignorance, to refrain from offending those among whom one has to live, and other such things regarding this inclination.

Article 3: Whether all acts of virtue belong to the natural law?

Objection 1: It would seem that not all acts of virtue belong to the natural law. Because, as was said above (90, 2,) it is essential to a law that it be ordered to the common good. But some acts of virtue

are ordered to the private good of the individual, as is especially clear
in regards to acts of temperance. Therefore not all acts of virtue are
subject to the natural law.

On the contrary, Damascene says (De Fide Orth.iii,4) that
'virtues are natural.' Therefore virtuous acts also are a subject of the
natural law.

We can speak of virtuous acts in two ways: first, insofar as they
are virtuous; secondly, as such and such acts considered in their
proper species. If then we speak of acts of virtue as virtuous, in this
way all virtuous acts pertain to the natural law. For it was said
(previous article) that to the natural law belongs everything to which
a man is inclined according to his nature. Now each thing is inclined
naturally to an operation that is suitable to it according to its form:
thus fire is inclined to give heat. Wherefore, since the rational soul is
the proper form of man, there is in every man a natural inclination to
act according to reason: and this is to act according to virtue.
Consequently, considered in this way, all acts of virtue belong to the
natural law: since everyone's reason naturally dictates to him to act
virtuously. But if we speak of virtuous acts in themselves, that is,
considered in their own species, in this way not all virtuous acts
belong to the natural law: for many things are done virtuously, to
which nature does not incline at first, but which, through the inquiry
of reason, have been found by men to be conducive to living well.

Reply To Objection 1: Temperance is about the natural desires
for food, drink, and sexual intercourse, which are certainly ordered to
the common good of nature, just as other matters of law are ordered
to the moral common good.

Article 4: Whether the natural law is the same for all?

Objection 2: "Things which are according to the law are said to be
just," as is said in the Ethics (V, 1). But it is stated in the same book
(V, 7) that nothing is so universally just as not to be subject to
change in regard to some men. Therefore even the natural law is not
the same for all.

Objection 3: Further, as was said above (previous two articles),
to the natural law belongs everything to which a man is inclined
according to his nature. Now different men are naturally inclined to

different things: some to desire for pleasures, others to desire for
220   honors, and other men to other things. Therefore there is not one
natural law for all.

On the contrary, Isidore says (Etym., V, 4): "The natural law is
common to all nations."

As stated above (previous two articles), to the natural law
225   belongs those things to which a man is inclined naturally: and among
these it is proper to man to be inclined to act according to reason.
Now it pertains to reason to proceed from the common to the proper,
as is clear from the Physics (I, 1). The speculative reason, however, is
differently situated in this matter from the practical reason.

230   For, since the speculative reason is busied chiefly with necessary
things, which cannot be otherwise than they are, its proper
conclusions, like the universal principles, contain the truth without
fail. The practical reason, on the other hand, is busied with
contingent matters, about which human actions are concerned: and
235   consequently, although there is necessity in the general principles,
the more we descend to matters of detail, the more frequently we
encounter defects. Accordingly then in speculative matters truth is
the same for all men, both as to principles and as to conclusions:
although the truth is not known by all as regards the conclusions,
240   but only as regards the principles which are called 'common notions'.
But in matters of action, truth or practical rectitude is not the same
for all, as to matters of detail, but only as to the general principles:
and where there is the same rectitude in matters of detail, it is not
equally known by all.

245   It is therefore evident that, as regards the general principles
whether of speculative or of practical reason, truth or rectitude is the
same for all, and is equally known by all.

As to the proper conclusions of the speculative reason, the truth
is the same for all, but is not equally known by all: thus it is true for
250   all that the three angles of a triangle are together equal to two right
angles, although it is not known by all. But as to the proper
conclusions of the practical reason, neither is the truth or rectitude
the same for all, nor, where it is the same, is it equally known by all.
Thus it is right and true for all to act according to reason: and from
255   this principle it follows as a proper conclusion that goods entrusted to
another should be restored to their owner. Now this is true for the

majority of cases: but it may happen in a particular case that it would be injurious, and therefore unreasonable, to restore goods held in trust; for instance, if they are claimed for the purpose of fighting against one's own country. And this principle will be found to fail the more, according as we descend further into detail, as if one were to say that goods held in trust should be restored with such and such a guarantee, or in such and such a way; because the greater the number of conditions added, the greater the number of ways in which the principle may fail, such that it might not be right to restore or not to restore.

Consequently we must say that the natural law, as to general principles, is the same for all, both as to rectitude and as to knowledge. But as to certain matters of detail, which are conclusions, as it were, of those general principles, it is the same for all for the most part both as to rectitude and as to knowledge; and yet in some few cases it may fail, both as to rectitude, by reason of certain obstacles (just as natures subject to generation and corruption fail in some few cases on account of some obstacle), and as to knowledge, since in some people reason is perverted by passion, or evil habit, or an evil disposition of nature; thus at one time theft, although it is expressly contrary to the natural law, was not considered wrong among the Germans, as Julius Caesar relates (De Bello Gallico, vi).

Reply To Objection 2: That statement of the Philosopher is to be understood of things that are naturally just, not as general principles, but as conclusions drawn from them, having rectitude for the most part, but failing in a few instances.

Reply To Objection 3: Just as, in man, reason rules and commands the other powers, so all the natural inclinations belonging to the other powers must be ordered according to reason. Wherefore it is universally right for all men, that all their inclinations should be directed according to reason.

Article 5: Whether the natural law can be changed?

A change in the natural law may be understood in two ways. First, by way of addition. In this sense nothing hinders the natural law from being changed: since many things for the benefit of human life have been added over and above the natural law, both by the Divine law and by human laws.

Secondly, a change in the natural law may be understood by way of subtraction, such that what previously was according to the natural law ceases to be so. In this sense, the natural law is altogether unchangeable in its first principles: but in its secondary principles, which, as we have said (previous article), are certain detailed proximate conclusions drawn from the first principles, the natural law is not changed such that what it prescribes is not right for the most part. But it may be changed in some particular cases of rare occurrence, through some special causes hindering the observance of such precepts, as was said above (previous article).

Article 6: Whether the natural law can be abolished from the heart of man?

Objection 1: It would seem that the natural law can be abolished from the heart of man. Because on Rm 2:14: "When the Gentiles who have not the law," and so forth, a gloss says that "the law of justice, which sin had blotted out, is inscribed on the heart of a man restored by grace." But the law of justice is the law of nature. Therefore the natural law can be blotted out.

Objection 3: Further, that which the law states becomes just, as it were. But many things are enacted by men which are contrary to natural law. Therefore the natural law can be abolished from the heart of man.

On the contrary, Augustine says (<u>Confessions</u>, ii): "Thy law is written in the hearts of men, which iniquity itself effaces not." But the law which is written in men's hearts is the natural law. Therefore the natural law cannot be blotted out.

As was said above (previous two articles), there belong to the natural law, first, certain most general precepts, which are known to all: and next, certain secondary and more detailed precepts, which are, as it were, conclusions following closely from these principles. As to the general principles, the natural law can in no way be altogether blotted out from men's hearts. But it may be blotted out in the case of a particular action, insofar as reason is hindered from applying the

general principle to a particular point of practice, on account of
concupiscence or some other passion, as was said above (77, 2).

But as to the other, secondary precepts, the natural law can be
blotted out from the human heart, either by evil persuasions, (just as
errors occur in speculative matters with respect to necessary
conclusions,) or by vicious customs and corrupt habits, as among
some men, theft, and even unnatural vices, were not deemed sinful,
as the Apostle says (Rm, i), .

Reply To Objection 1: Sin blots out the natural law in particular
cases, not universally, except perhaps in regard to the secondary
precepts of the natural law, in the manner stated above.

Reply To Objection 3: This argument is true of the secondary
precepts of the natural law, against which some legislators have
framed certain enactments which are unjust.

QUESTION NINETY-FIVE

OF HUMAN LAW

Article 2: Whether every human law is derived from the natural law?

Objection 1: It would seem that not every human law is derived
from the natural law. For the Philosopher says (Ethics, V, 7) that
"the legally just is that which originally was indifferent." But those
things which arise from the natural law are not matters of
indifference. Therefore the statutes of human laws are not all derived
from the natural law.

Objection 3: Further, the natural law is the same for all; for the
Philosopher says (Ethics, V, 7) that "what is naturally just is that
which everywhere has the same force." If therefore human laws were
derived from the natural law, it would follow that they too are the
same for all: which is clearly false.

On the contrary, Tully [Cicero] says (Rhetor., ii): "Things which
emanated from nature and were approved by custom, were
sanctioned by fear and reverence for the laws."

As Augustine says (De Lib.Arb., i, 5) "that which is not just
seems to be no law at all:" wherefore the force of a law depends on
the extent of its justice. Now in human affairs a thing is said to be

355   just from being right, according to the rule of reason. But the first rule
        of reason is the natural law, as is clear from what has been said
        above (91, 2, <u>ad</u> 2). Consequently every human law has just so much
        of the nature of law as it is derived from the natural law. But if it is
        discordant with the natural law in some respect, it is no longer a law
360   but a corruption of law.

        Yet it must be noted that something may be derived from the
        natural law in two ways: first, as a conclusion from premises,
        secondly, by way of determination of certain generalities. The first
        way is similar to that by which, in the sciences, demonstrated
365   conclusions are drawn from the principles: while the second way is
        similar to that whereby, in the arts, general forms are particularized
        as to details: thus the craftsman needs to determine the general form
        of a house to some particular shape.

        Some things are therefore derived from the general principles of
370   the natural law by way of conclusions: for example, 'do not kill' may
        be derived as a conclusion from the principle 'do harm to no one':
        while others are derived by way of determination: for example, the
        law of nature has it that he who does evil should be punished; but
        that he be punished in this or that way is a determination of the law
375   of nature.

        Consequently, both modes of derivation are found in the human
        law. But those things which are derived in the first way [as
        conclusions] are contained in human law not solely as emanating
        from it, rather they have some of their force from the natural law
380   also. But those things which are derived in the second way have no
        other force than that of human law.

        Reply To Objection 1: The Philosopher is speaking of those
        enactments which are by way of determination or specification of the
        precepts of the natural law.

385   Reply To Objection 3: The general principles of the natural law
        cannot be applied to all in the same way on account of the great
        variety of human affairs: and hence arises the diversity of positive
        laws among various people.

Thomas Hobbes, *Leviathan*

CHAPTER XIII—OF THE NATURAL CONDITION OF MANKIND AS CONCERNING THEIR FELICITY, AND MISERY

Nature has made men so equal, in the faculties of the body and mind; as that, though there be found one man sometimes manifestly stronger in body or of quicker mind than another, yet when all is reckoned together, the difference between man and man is not so considerable, as that one man can thereupon claim to himself any benefit, to which another may not pretend as well as he. For as to the strength of the body, the weakest has strength enough to kill the strongest, whether by secret machination, or by confederacy with others that are in the same danger with himself.

And as to the faculties of the mind setting aside the arts grounded upon words, and especially that skill of proceeding upon general and infallible rules, called science; which very few have, and but in few things; as being not a native faculty, born with us; nor attained, as prudence, while we look after somewhat else I find yet a greater equality amongst men, than that of strength. For prudence is but experience, which equal time equally bestows on all men, in those things they equally apply themselves unto. That which may perhaps make such equality incredible, is but a vain conceit of one s own wisdom, which almost all men think they have in a greater degree than the vulgar; that is, than all men but themselves, and a few others, whom by fame, or for concurring with themselves, they approve. For such is the nature of men, that howsoever they may acknowledge many others to be more witty, or more eloquent, or more learned, yet they will hardly believe there be many so wise as themselves; for they see their own wit at hand, and other men s at a distance. But this proves rather that men are in that point equal, than unequal. For there is not ordinarily a greater sign of the equal distribution of anything, than that every man is contented with his share.

From this equality of ability, arises equality of hope in the attaining of our ends. And therefore if any two men desire the same thing, which nevertheless they cannot both enjoy, they become enemies; and in the way to their end, which is principally their own

conservation, and sometimes their delectation only, endeavor to
35   destroy, or subdue one another. And from hence it comes to pass that
where an invader has no more to fear than another man s single
power; if one plant, sow, build, or possess a convenient seat, others
may probably be expected to come prepared with forces united, to
dispossess and deprive him, not only of the fruit of his labor, but also
40   of his life or liberty. And the invader again is in the like danger of
another.

And from this diffidence of one another, there is no way for any
man to secure himself so reasonable as anticipation; that is, by force
or wiles to master the persons of all men he can, so long, till he sees
45   no other power great enough to endanger him: and this is no more
than his own conservation requires, and is generally allowed. Also
because there be some, that taking pleasure in contemplating their
own power in the acts of conquest, which they pursue farther than
their security requires; if others, that otherwise would be glad to be
50   at ease within modest bounds, should not by invasion increase their
power, they would not be able long time, by standing only on their
defense, to subsist. And by consequence, such augmentation of
dominion over men being necessary to a man s conservation, it ought
to be allowed him.

55   Again, men have no pleasure, but on the contrary a great deal of
grief, in keeping company, where there is no power able to overawe
them all. For every man looks that his companion should value him
at the same rate he sets upon himself; and upon all signs of
contempt, or undervaluing, naturally endeavors, as far as he dares
60   (which amongst them that have no common power to keep them in
quiet, is far enough to make them destroy each other), to extort a
greater value from his contemners by damage, and from others by the
example.

So that in the nature of man, we find three principal causes of
65   quarrel. First, competition; second, diffidence; thirdly, glory.

The first makes men invade for gain; the second, for safety; and
the third, for reputation. The first use violence to make themselves
masters of other men s persons, wives, children, and cattle; the
second, to defend them; the third, for trifles, as a word, a smile, a
70   different opinion, and any other sign of undervalue, either direct in

their persons, or by reflection in their kindred, their friends, their nation, their profession, or their name.

Hereby it is manifest that during the time men live without a common power to keep them all in awe, they are in that condition which is called war; and such a war as is of every man against every man. For war consists not in battle only, or the act of fighting, but in a tract of time wherein the will to contend by battle is sufficiently known, and therefore the notion of time is to be considered in the nature of war, as it is in the nature of weather. For as the nature of foul weather lies not in a shower or two of rain, but in an inclination thereto of many days together; so the nature of war consists not in actual fighting, but in the known disposition thereto, during all the time there is no assurance to the contrary. All other time is peace.

Whatsoever therefore is consequent to the time of war, where every man is enemy to every man; the same is consequent to the time, wherein men live without other security than what their own strength and their own invention shall furnish them withal. In such condition there is no place for industry, because the fruit thereof is uncertain: and consequently no culture of the earth; no navigation, nor use of the commodities that may be imported by sea; no commodious building; no instruments of moving, and removing, such things as require much force; no knowledge of the face of the earth; no account of time; no arts; no letters; no society; and which is worst of all, continual fear, and danger of violent death; and the life of man, solitary, poor, nasty, brutish, and short.

It may seem strange to some man that has not well weighed these things, that nature should thus dissociate, and render men apt to invade and destroy one another; and he may therefore, not trusting to this inference, made from the passions, desire perhaps to have the same confirmed by experience. Let him therefore consider with himself, when taking a journey, he arms himself and seeks to go well accompanied; when going to sleep, he locks his doors; when even in his house he locks his chests; and this when he knows there be laws, and public officers, armed, to revenge all injuries shall be done him: what opinion he has of his fellow-subjects, when he rides armed; of his fellow-citizens, when he locks his doors; and of his children, and servants, when he locks his chests. Does he not here as much accuse mankind by his actions, as I do by my words? But

neither of us accuse man s nature in it. The desires, and other
110   passions of man, are in themselves no sin. No more are the actions
that proceed from those passions, till they know a law that forbids
them: which till laws be made they cannot know; nor can any law be
made, till they have agreed upon the person that shall make it.

It may peradventure be thought, there was never such a time nor
115   condition of war as this; and I believe it was never generally so, over
all the world: but there are many places where they live so now. For
the savage people in many places of America, except the government
of small families, the concord whereof depends on natural lust, have
no government at all; and live at this day in that brutish manner, as
120   I said before. Howsoever, it may be perceived what manner of life
there would be, where there were no common power to fear; by the
manner of life which men that have formerly lived under a peaceful
government, use to degenerate into in a civil war.

But though there had never been any time wherein particular
125   men were in a condition of war one against another; yet in all times,
kings, and persons of sovereign authority, because of their
independency, are in continual jealousies, and in the state and
posture of gladiators; having their weapons pointing, and their eyes
fixed on one another; that is, their forts, garrisons, and guns upon
130   the frontiers of their kingdoms; and continual spies upon their
neighbors; which is a posture of war. But because they uphold
thereby the industry of their subjects, there does not follow from it
that misery which accompanies the liberty of particular men.

To this war of every man against every man, this also is
135   consequent: that nothing can be unjust. The notions of right and
wrong, justice and injustice, have there no place. Where there is no
common power, there is no law; where no law, no injustice. Force and
fraud are in war the two cardinal virtues. Justice and injustice are
none of the faculties neither of the body nor mind. If they were, they
140   might be in a man that were alone in the world, as well as his
senses and passions. They are qualities that relate to men in society,
not in solitude. It is consequent also to the same condition, that
there be no propriety, no dominion, no mine and thine distinct; but
only that to be every man s, that he can get; and for so long as he can
145   keep it. And thus much for the ill condition which man by mere

nature is actually placed in; though with a possibility to come out of it, consisting partly in the passions, partly in his reason.

The passions that incline men to peace are fear of death, desire of such things as are necessary to commodious living, and a hope by their industry to obtain them. And reason suggests convenient articles of peace, upon which men may be drawn to agreement. These articles are they which otherwise are called the Laws of Nature whereof I shall speak more particularly in the two following chapters.

CHAPTER XIV—THE FIRST AND SECOND NATURAL LAWS, AND OF CONTRACTS

The right of nature, which writers commonly call *jus naturale*, is the liberty each man has to use his own power, as he will himself, for the preservation of his own nature; that is to say, of his own life; and consequently, of doing anything, which in his own judgment and reason, he shall conceive to be the aptest means thereunto.

By liberty, is understood, according to the proper signification of the word, the absence of external impediments: which impediments, may oft take away part of a man power to do what he would; but cannot hinder him from using the power left him, according as his judgment and reason shall dictate to him.

A law of nature, *lex naturalis*, is a precept or general rule, found out by reason, by which a man is forbidden to do that which is destructive of his life, or takes away the means of preserving the same; and to omit that by which he thinks it may be best preserved. For though they that speak of this subject, use to confound *jus* and *lex*, right and law; yet they ought to be distinguished: because right consists in liberty to do or to forbear, whereas law determines and binds to one of them; so that law, and right differ as much as obligation and liberty; which in one and the same matter are inconsistent.

And because the condition of man, as has been declared in the precedent chapter, is a condition of war of everyone against everyone; in which case everyone is governed by his own reason, and there is nothing he can make use of that may not be a help unto him in preserving his life against his enemies: it follows, that in such a condition every man has a right to everything; even to one another's body. And therefore, as long as this natural right of every man to everything endures, there can be no security to any man, how strong or wise soever he be, of living out the time which nature ordinarily allows men to live. And consequently it is a precept, or general rule of

185   reason, that every man ought to endeavor peace, as far as he has hope of obtaining it; and when he cannot obtain it, that he may seek and use all helps and advantages of war. The first branch of which rule contains the first and fundamental law of nature; which is, to seek peace and follow it. The second, the sum of the right of nature;

190   which is, by all means we can, to defend ourselves.

From this fundamental law of nature, by which men are commanded to endeavor peace, is derived this second law: that a man be willing, when others are so too, as far forth as for peace and defense of himself he shall think it necessary, to lay down this right

195   to all things; and be contented with so much liberty against other men, as he would allow other men against himself. For as long as every man holds this right, of doing anything he likes, so long are all men in the condition of war. But if other men will not lay down their right, as well as he, then there is no reason for anyone to divest

200   himself of his: for that were to expose himself to prey, which no man is bound to, rather than to dispose himself to peace. This is that law of the Gospel: whatsoever you require that others should do to you, that do you to them. And that law of all men, *quod tibi fieri non vis, alteri ne feceris.*

205   To lay down a man's right to anything, is to divest himself of the liberty, of hindering another of the benefit of his own right to the same. For he that renounces or passes away his right, gives not to any other man a right which he had not before; because there is nothing to which every man had not right by nature: but only stands

210   out of his way, that he may enjoy his own original right, without hindrance from him, not without hindrance from another. So that the effect which redounds to one man, by another man s defect of right, is but so much diminution of impediments to the use of his own right original.

215   Right is laid aside, either by simply renouncing it, or by transferring it to another. By simply renouncing, when he cares not to whom the benefit thereof redounds. By transferring, when he intends the benefit thereof to some certain person or persons. And when a

man has in either manner abandoned or granted away his right;
220   then is he said to be obliged, or bound, not to hinder those to whom
such right is granted or abandoned, from the benefit of it; and that
he ought, and it is his duty, not to make void that voluntary act of
his own; and that such hindrance is injustice, and injury, as being
sine jure; the right being before renounced, or transferred. So that
225   injury, or injustice in the controversies of the world, is somewhat like
to that, which in the disputations of scholars is called absurdity. For
as it is there called an absurdity to contradict what one maintained
in the beginning; so in the world, it is called injustice, and injury,
voluntarily to undo that which from the beginning he had voluntarily
230   done. The way by which a man either simply renounces, or transfers
his right, is a declaration, or signification, by some voluntary and
sufficient sign or signs, that he renounces or transfers or has
renounced or transferred the same, to him that accepts it. And these
signs are either words only, or actions only, or, as it happens most
235   often, both words and actions. And the same are the bonds, by which
men are bound and obliged—bonds that have their strength, not
from their own nature, for nothing is more easily broken than a man
s word, but from fear of some evil consequence upon the rupture.

Whenever a man transfers his right, or renounces, it; it is either
240   in consideration of some right reciprocally transferred to himself, or
for some other good he hopes for thereby. For it is a voluntary act;
and of the voluntary acts of every man, the object is some good to
himself. And therefor there be some rights which no man can be
understood by any words, or other signs, to have abandoned or
245   transferred. As first a man cannot lay down the right of resisting
them that assault him by force, to take away his life; because he
cannot be understood to aim thereby, at any good to himself. The
same may be said of wounds, and chains, and imprisonment: both
because there is no benefit consequent to such patience, as there is to
250   the patience of suffering another to be wounded or imprisoned; as
also because a man cannot tell, when he sees men proceed against
him by violence, whether they intend his death or not. And lastly the
motive, and end for which this renouncing and transferring of right is
introduced, is nothing else but the security of a man s person, in his
255   life, and in the means of so preserving life as not to be weary of it.
And therefore if a man by words, or other signs, seem to despoil

himself of the end for which those signs were intended, he is not to be understood as if he meant it, or that it was his will, but that he was ignorant of how such words and actions were to be interpreted.

260   The mutual transferring of right, is that which men call contract.

When the transferring of right is not mutual; but one of the parties transfers, in hope to gain thereby friendship, or service from another, or from his friends; or in hope to gain the reputation of charity, or magnanimity; or to deliver his mind from the pain of

265   compassion; or in hope of reward in heaven; this is not contract, but gift, free-gift, grace: which words signify one and the same thing.

He that performs first in the case of a contract, is said to merit that which he is to receive by the performance of the other; and he has it as due. Also when a prize is propounded to many, which is to

270   be given to him only that wins; or money is thrown among many, to be enjoyed by them that catch it; though this be a free gift; yet so to win, or so to catch is to merit, and to have it as due. For the right is transferred in the propounding of the prize, and in throwing down the money; though it be not determined to whom, but by the event of the

275   contention.

If a covenant be made, wherein neither of the parties perform presently, but trust one another; in the condition of mere nature, which is a condition of war of every man against every man, upon any reasonable suspicion, it is void: but if there be a common power set

280   over them both, with right and force sufficient to compel performance, it is not void. For he that performs first, has no assurance the other will perform after; because the bonds of words are too weak to bridle men s ambition, avarice, anger, and other passions, without the fear of some coercive power; which in the condition of mere nature, where

285   all men are equal, and judges of the justness of their own fears, cannot possibly be supposed. And therefore he which performs first, does but betray himself to his enemy; contrary to the right, he can never abandon, of defending his life, and means of living.

But in a civil estate, where there is a power set up to constrain

290   those that would otherwise violate their faith, that fear is no more reasonable; and for that cause, he which by the covenant is to perform first, is obliged so to do.

David Hume, *Treatise on Human Nature*

BOOK III: OF MORALS

PART I: OF VIRTUE AND VICE IN GENERAL

SECTION I: MORAL DISTINCTIONS NOT DERIVED FROM REASON

5   There is an inconvenience which attends all abstruse reasoning. that it may silence, without convincing an antagonist, and requires the same intense study to make us sensible of its force, that was at first requisite for its invention. When we leave our closet, and engage in the common affairs of life, its conclusions seem to vanish, like the
10   phantoms of the night on the appearance of the morning; and it is difficult for us to retain even that conviction, which we had attained with difficulty. This is still more conspicuous in a long chain of reasoning, where we must preserve to the end the evidence of the first propositions, and where we often lose sight of ail the most
15   received maxims, either of philosophy or common life. I am not, however, without hopes, that the present system of philosophy will acquire new force as it advances; and that our reasonings concerning morals will corroborate whatever has been said concerning the understanding and the passions. Morality is a subject that interests
20   us above all others: We fancy the peace of society to be at stake in every decision concerning it; and it is evident, that this concern must make our speculations appear more real and solid, than where the subject is, in a great measure, indifferent to us. What affects us, we conclude can never be a chimera; and as our passion is engaged on
25   the one side or the other, we naturally think that the question lies within human comprehension; which, in other cases of this nature, we are apt to entertain some doubt of. Without this advantage I never should have ventured upon a third volume of such abstruse philosophy, in an age, wherein the greatest part of men seem agreed
30   to convert reading into an amusement, and to reject every thing that requires any considerable degree of attention to be comprehended.

    It has been observed, that nothing is ever present to the mind but its perceptions; and that all the actions of seeing, hearing,

judging, loving, hating, and thinking, fall under this denomination.
35   The mind can never exert itself in any action, which we may not
comprehend under the term of perception; and consequently that
term is no less applicable to those judgments, by which we
distinguish moral good and evil, than to every other operation of the
mind. To approve of one character, to condemn another, are only so
40   many different perceptions.

Now as perceptions resolve themselves into two kinds, viz.
impressions and ideas, this distinction gives rise to a question, with
which we shall open up our present inquiry concerning morals.
Whether it is by means of our ideas or impressions we distinguish
45   betwixt vice and virtue, and pronounce an action blamable or
praiseworthy? This will immediately cut off all loose discourses and
declamations, and reduce us to something precise and exact on the
present subject.

Those who affirm that virtue is nothing but a conformity to
50   reason; that there are eternal fitnesses and unfitnesses of things,
which are the same to every rational being that considers them; that
the immutable measures of right and wrong impose an obligation,
not only on human creatures, but also on the Deity himself: All these
systems concur in the opinion, that morality, like truth, is discerned
55   merely by ideas, and by their juxtaposition and comparison. In order,
therefore, to judge of these systems, we need only consider, whether
it be possible, from reason alone, to distinguish betwixt moral good
and evil, or whether there must concur some other principles to
enable us to make that distinction.

60   If morality had naturally no influence on human passions and
actions, it were in vain to take such pains to inculcate it; and nothing
would be more fruitless than that multitude of rules and precepts,
with which all moralists abound. Philosophy is commonly divided
into speculative and practical; and as morality is always
65   comprehended under the latter division, it is supposed to influence
our passions and actions, and to go beyond the calm and indolent
judgments of the understanding. And this is confirmed by common
experience, which informs us, that men are often governed by their
duties, and are deterred from some actions by the opinion of
70   injustice, and impelled to others by that of obligation.

Since morals, therefore, have an influence on the actions and affections, it follows, that they cannot be derived from reason; and that because reason alone, as we have already proved, can never have any such influence. Morals excite passions, and produce or
75 prevent actions. Reason of itself is utterly impotent in this particular. The rules of morality. therefore, are not conclusions of our reason.

No one, I believe, will deny the justness of this inference; nor is there any other means of evading it, than by denying that principle, on which it is founded. As long as it is allowed, that reason has no
80 influence on our passions and action., it is in vain to pretend, that morality is discovered only by a deduction of reason. An active principle can never be founded on an inactive; and if reason be inactive in itself, it must remain so in all its shapes and appearances, whether it exerts itself in natural or moral subjects,
85 whether it considers the powers of external bodies, or the actions of rational beings.

It would be tedious to repeat all the arguments, by which I have proved, that reason is perfectly inert, and can never either prevent or produce any action or affection. `Twill be easy to recollect what has
90 been said upon that subject. I shall only recall on this occasion one of these arguments, which I shall endeavor to render still more conclusive, and more applicable to the present subject.

Reason is the discovery of truth or falsehood. Truth or falsehood consists in an agreement or disagreement either to the real relations
95 of ideas, or to real existence and matter of fact. Whatever, therefore, is not susceptible of this agreement or disagreement, is incapable of being true or false, and can never be an object of our reason. Now it is evident our passions, volitions, and actions, are not susceptible of any such agreement or disagreement; being original facts and
100 realities, complete in themselves, and implying no reference to other passions, volitions, and actions. It is impossible, therefore, they can be pronounced either true or false, and be either contrary or conformable to reason.

This argument is of double advantage to our present purpose.
105 For it proves directly, that actions do not derive their merit from a conformity to reason, nor their blame from a contrariety to it; and it proves the same truth more indirectly, by showing us, that as reason can never immediately prevent or produce any action by contradicting

or approving of it, it cannot be the source of moral good and evil,
110   which are found to have that influence. Actions may be laudable or
blamable; but they cannot be reasonable: Laudable or blamable,
therefore, are not the same with reasonable or unreasonable. The
merit and demerit of actions frequently contradict, and sometimes
control our natural propensities. But reason has no such influence.
115   Moral distinctions, therefore, are not the offspring of reason. Reason
is wholly inactive, and can never be the source of so active a principle
as conscience, or a sense of morals. ...

But to make these general reflections more clear and convincing,
we may illustrate them by some particular instances, wherein this
120   character of moral good or evil is the most universally acknowledged.
Of all crimes that human creatures are capable of committing, the
most horrid and unnatural is ingratitude, especially when it is
committed against parents, and appears in the more flagrant
instances of wounds and death. This is acknowledged by all
125   mankind, philosophers as well as the people; the question only
arises among philosophers, whether the guilt or moral deformity of
this action be discovered by demonstrative reasoning, or be felt by an
internal sense, and by means of some sentiment, which the reflecting
on such an action naturally occasions. This question will soon be
130   decided against the former opinion, if we can show the same
relations in other objects, without the notion of any guilt or iniquity
attending them. Reason or science is nothing but the comparing of
ideas, and the discovery of their relations; and if the same relations
have different characters, it must evidently follow, that those
135   characters are not discovered merely by reason. To put the affair,
therefore, to this trial, let us choose any inanimate object, such as an
oak or elm; and let us suppose, that by the dropping of its seed, it
produces a sapling below it, which springing up by degrees, at last
overtops and destroys the parent tree: I ask, if in this instance there
140   be wanting any relation, which is discoverable in parricide or
ingratitude? Is not the one tree the cause of the other's existence; and
the latter the cause of the destruction of the former, in the same
manner as when a child murders his parent? It is not sufficient to
reply, that a choice or will is wanting. For in the case of parricide, a
145   will does not give rise to any different relations, but is only the cause
from which the action is derived; and consequently produces the

same relations, that in the oak or elm arise from some other principles. it is a will or choice, that determines a man to kill his parent; and they are the laws of matter and motion, that determine a sapling to destroy the oak, from which it sprung. Here then the same relations have different causes; but still the relations are the same: And as their discovery is not in both cases attended with a notion of immorality, it follows, that that notion does not arise from such a discovery.

But to choose an instance, still more resembling; I would fain ask any one, why incest in the human species is criminal, and why the very same action, and the same relations in animals have not the smallest moral turpitude and deformity? If it be answered, that this action is innocent in animals, because they have not reason sufficient to discover its turpitude; but that man, being endowed with that faculty which ought to restrain him to his duty, the same action instantly becomes criminal to him; should this be said, I would reply, that this is evidently arguing in a circle. For before reason can perceive this turpitude, the turpitude must exist; and consequently is independent of the decisions of our reason, and is their object more properly than their effect. According to this system, then, every animal, that has sense, and appetite, and will; that is, every animal must be susceptible of all the same virtues and vices, for which we ascribe praise and blame to human creatures. All the difference is, that our superior reason may serve to discover the vice or virtue, and by that means may augment the blame or praise: But still this discovery supposes a separate being in these moral distinctions, and a being, which depends only on the will and appetite, and which, both in thought and reality, may be distinguished from the reason. Animals are susceptible of the same relations, with respect to each other, as the human species, and therefore would also be susceptible of the same morality, if the essence of morality consisted in these relations. Their want of a sufficient degree of reason may hinder them from perceiving the duties and obligations of morality, but can never hinder these duties from existing; since they must antecedently exist, in order to their being perceived. Reason must find them, and can never produce them. This argument deserves to be weighed, as being, in my opinion, entirely decisive.

Nor does this reasoning only prove, that morality consists not in
any relations, that are the objects of science; but if examined, will
prove with equal certainty, that it consists not in any matter of fact,
which can be discovered by the understanding. This is the second
part of our argument; and if it can be made evident, we may
conclude, that morality is not an object of reason. But can there be
any difficulty in proving, that vice and virtue are not matters of fact,
whose existence we can infer by reason? Take any action allowed to
be vicious: Willful murder, for instance. Examine it in all lights, and
see if you can find that matter of fact, or real existence, which you call
vice. In whichever way you take it, you find only certain passions,
motives, volitions and thoughts. There is no other matter of fact in
the case. The vice entirely escapes you, as long as you consider the
object. You never can find it, till you turn your reflection into your own
breast, and find a sentiment of disapprobation, which arises in you,
towards this action. Here is a matter of fact; but it is the object of
feeling, not of reason. It lies in yourself, not in the object. So that
when you pronounce any action or character to be vicious, you mean
nothing, but that from the constitution of your nature you have a
feeling or sentiment of blame from the contemplation of it. Vice and
virtue, therefore, may be compared to sounds, colors, heat and cold,
which, according to modern philosophy, are not qualities in objects,
but perceptions in the mind: And this discovery in morals, like that
other in physics, is to be regarded as a considerable advancement of
the speculative sciences; though, like that too, it has little or no
influence on practice. Nothing can be more real, or concern us more,
than our own sentiments of pleasure and uneasiness; and if these be
favorable to virtue, and unfavorable to vice, no more can be requisite
to the regulation of our conduct and behavior.

I cannot forbear adding to these reasonings an observation,
which may, perhaps, be found of some importance. In every system of
morality, which I have hitherto met with, I have always remarked,
that the author proceeds for some time in the ordinary way of
reasoning, and establishes the being of a God, or makes observations
concerning human affairs; when of a sudden I am surprised to find,
that instead of the usual copulations of propositions, is, and is not, I
meet with no proposition that is not connected with an ought, or an
ought not. This change is imperceptible; but is, however, of the last

consequence. For as this ought, or ought not, expresses some new relation or affirmation, it is necessary that it should be observed and explained; and at the same time that a reason should be given, for

225 what seems altogether inconceivable, how this new relation can be a deduction from others, which are entirely different from it. But as authors do not commonly use this precaution, I shall presume to recommend it to the readers; and am persuaded, that this small attention would subvert all the vulgar systems of morality, and let us

230 see, that the distinction of vice and virtue is not founded merely on the relations of objects, nor is perceived by reason.

SECTION II: MORAL DISTINCTIONS DERIVED FROM A MORAL SENSE

Thus the course of the argument leads us to conclude, that since vice and virtue are not discoverable merely by reason, or the

235 comparison of ideas, it must be by means of some impression or sentiment they occasion, that we are able to mark the difference betwixt them. Our decisions concerning moral rectitude and depravity are evidently perceptions; and as all perceptions are either impressions or ideas, the exclusion of the one is a convincing

240 argument for the other. Morality, therefore, is more properly felt than judged of; though this feeling or sentiment is commonly so soft and gentle, that we are apt to confound it with an idea, according to our common custom of taking all things for the same, which have any near resemblance to each other.

245 The next question is, Of what nature are these impressions, and after what manner do they operate upon us? Here we cannot remain long in suspense, but must pronounce the impression arising from virtue, to be agreeable, and that proceeding from vice to be uneasy. Every moments experience must convince us of this. There is no

250 spectacle so fair and beautiful as a noble and generous action; nor any which gives us more abhorrence than one that is cruel and treacherous. No enjoyment. equals the satisfaction we receive from the company of those we love and esteem; as the greatest of all punishments is to be obliged to pass our lives with those we hate or

255 contemn. A very play or romance may afford us instances of this

pleasure, which virtue conveys to us; and pain, which arises from
vice.

260

265

270

275

280

285

290

Now since the distinguishing impressions, by which moral good or
evil is known, are nothing but particular pains or pleasures; it
follows, that in all inquiries concerning these moral distinctions, it
will be sufficient to show the principles, which make us feel a
satisfaction or uneasiness from the survey of any character, in order
to satisfy us why the character is laudable or blamable. An action, or
sentiment, or character is virtuous or vicious; why? because its view
causes a pleasure or uneasiness of a particular kind. In giving a
reason, therefore, for the pleasure or uneasiness, we sufficiently
explain the vice or virtue. To have the sense of virtue, is nothing but
to feel a satisfaction of a particular kind from the contemplation of a
character. The very feeling constitutes our praise or admiration. We
go no farther; nor do we inquire into the cause of the satisfaction. We
do not infer a character to be virtuous, because it pleases: But in
feeling that it pleases after such a particular manner, we in effect feel
that it is virtuous. The case is the same as in our judgments
concerning all kinds of beauty, and tastes, and sensations. Our
approbation is implied in the immediate pleasure they convey to us.

I have objected to the system, which establishes eternal rational
measures of right and wrong, that it is impossible to show, in the
actions of reasonable creatures, any relations, which are not found in
external objects; and therefore, if morality always attended these
relations, it were possible for inanimate matter to become virtuous or
vicious. Now it may, in like manner, be objected to the present
system, that if virtue and vice be determined by pleasure and pain,
these qualities must, in every case, arise from the sensations; and
consequently any object, whether animate or inanimate, rational or
irrational, might become morally good or evil, provided it can excite a
satisfaction or uneasiness. But though this objection seems to be the
very same, it has by no means the same force, in the one case as in
the other. For, first, it is evident, that under the term pleasure, we
comprehend sensations, which are very different from each other, and
which have only such a distant resemblance, as is requisite to make
them be expressed by the same abstract term. A good composition of
music and a bottle of good wine equally produce pleasure; and what
is more, their goodness is determined merely by the pleasure. But

295 shall we say upon that account, that the wine is harmonious, or the music of a good flavor? In like manner an inanimate object, and the character or sentiments of any person may, both of them, give satisfaction; but as the satisfaction is different, this keeps our sentiments concerning them from being confounded, and makes us ascribe virtue to the one, and not to the other. Nor is every sentiment 300 of pleasure or pain, which arises from characters and actions, of that peculiar kind, which makes us praise or condemn. The good qualities of an enemy are hurtful to us; but may still command our esteem and respect. it is only when a character is considered in general, without reference to our particular interest, that it causes such a feeling or 305 sentiment, as denominates it morally good or evil. it is true, those sentiments, from interest and morals, are apt to be confounded, and naturally run into one another. It seldom happens, that we do not think an enemy vicious, and can distinguish betwixt his opposition to our interest and real villainy or baseness. But this hinders not, but 310 that the sentiments are, in themselves, distinct; and a man of temper and judgment may preserve himself from these illusions. In like manner, though it is certain a musical voice is nothing but one that naturally gives a particular kind of pleasure; yet it is difficult for a man to be sensible, that the voice of an enemy is agreeable, or to 315 allow it to be musical. But a person of a fine ear, who has the command of himself, can separate these feelings, and give praise to what deserves it. ...

Meanwhile it may not be amiss to observe from these definitions of natural and unnatural, that nothing can be more unphilosophical 320 than those systems, which assert, that virtue is the same with what is natural, and vice with what is unnatural. For in the first sense of the word, Nature, as opposed to miracles, both vice and virtue are equally natural; and in the second sense, as opposed to what is unusual, perhaps virtue will be found to be the most unnatural. At 325 least it must be owned, that heroic virtue, being as unusual, is as little natural as the most brutal barbarity. As to the third sense of the word, it is certain, that both vice and virtue are equally artificial, and out of nature. For however it may be disputed, whether the notion of a merit or demerit in certain actions be natural or artificial, 330 it is evident, that the actions themselves are artificial, and are performed with a certain design and intention; otherwise they could never be ranked under any of these denominations. It is impossible, therefore, that the character of natural and unnatural can ever, in any sense, mark the boundaries of vice and virtue.

335   Thus we are still brought back to our first position, that virtue is distinguished by the pleasure, and vice by the pain, that any action, sentiment or character gives us by the mere view and contemplation. This decision is very commodious; because it reduces us to this simple question, Why any action or sentiment upon the general view

340   or survey, gives a certain satisfaction or uneasiness, in order to show the origin of its moral rectitude or depravity, without looking for any incomprehensible relations and qualities, which never did exist in nature, nor even in our imagination, by any clear and distinct conception. I flatter myself I have executed a great part of my present

345   design by a state of the question, which appears to me so free from ambiguity and obscurity. ... We may begin with considering anew the nature and force of sympathy. The minds of all men are similar in their feelings and operations; nor can any one be actuated by any affection, of which all others are not, in some degree, susceptible. As

350   in strings equally wound up, the motion of one communicates itself to the rest; so all the affections readily pass from one person to another, and beget correspondent movements in every human creature. When I see the effects of passion in the voice and gesture of any person, my mind immediately passes from these effects to their causes, and

355   forms such a lively idea of the passion, as is presently converted into the passion itself. In like manner, when I perceive the causes of any emotion, my mind is conveyed to the effects, and is actuated with a like emotion. Were I present at any of the more terrible operations of surgery, it is certain, that even before it begun, the preparation of the

360   instruments, the laying of the bandages in order, the heating of the irons, with all the signs of anxiety and concern in the patient and assistants, would have a great effect upon my mind, and excite the strongest sentiments of pity and terror. No passion of another discovers itself immediately to the mind. We are only sensible of its

365   causes or effects. From these we infer the passion: And consequently these give rise to our sympathy.

Immanuel Kant, *Fundamental Principles of the Metaphysics of Morals*

FIRST SECTION—TRANSITION FROM THE COMMON RATIONAL KNOWLEDGE OF MORALITY TO THE PHILOSOPHICAL

Nothing can possibly be conceived in the world, or even out of it, which can be called good without qualification, except a Good Will. Intelligence, wit, judgment, and the other talents of the mind, however they may be named, or courage, resolution, perseverance, as
5 qualities of temperament, are undoubtedly good and desirable in many respects; but these gifts of nature may also become extremely bad and mischievous if the will which is to make use of them, and which, therefore, constitutes what is called character, is not good. It is the same with the gifts of fortune. Power, riches, honor, even
10 health, and the general well-being and contentment with one's condition which is called happiness, inspire pride, and often presumption, if there is not a good will to correct the influence of these on the mind, and with this also to rectify the whole principle of acting, and adapt it to its end. The sight of a being who is not
15 adorned with a single feature of a pure and good will, enjoying unbroken prosperity, can never give pleasure to an impartial rational spectator. Thus a good will appears to constitute the indispensable condition even of being worthy of happiness.

There are even some qualities which are of service to this good
20 will itself, and may facilitate its action, yet which have no intrinsic unconditional value, but always presuppose a good will, and this qualifies the esteem that we justly have for them, and does not permit us to regard them as absolutely good. Moderation in the affections and passions, self-control and calm deliberation are not
25 only good in many respects, but even seem to constitute part of the intrinsic worth of the person; but they are far from deserving to be called good without qualification, although they have been so unconditionally praised by the ancients. For without the principles of a good will, they may become extremely bad, and the coolness of a
30 villain not only makes him far more dangerous, but also directly

makes him more abominable in our eyes than he would have been without it.

A good will is good not because of what it performs or effects, not by its aptness for the attainment of some proposed end, but simply by virtue of the volition, that is, it is good in itself, and considered by itself is to be esteemed much higher than all that can be brought about by it in favor of any inclination, nay, even of the sum total of all inclinations. Even if it should happen that, owing to special disfavor of fortune, or the niggardly provision of a step-motherly nature, this will should wholly lack power to accomplish its purpose, if with its greatest efforts it should yet achieve nothing, and there should remain only the good will (not, to be sure, a mere wish, but the summoning of all means in our power), then, like a jewel, it would still shine by its own light, as a thing which has its whole value in itself. It s usefulness or fruitlessness can neither add to nor take away anything from this value. It would be, as it were, only the setting to enable us to handle it the more conveniently in common commerce or to attract to it the attention of those who are not yet connoisseurs, but not to recommend it to true connoisseurs, or to determine its value. ...

We have then to develop the notion of a will which deserves to be highly esteemed for itself, and is good without a view to anything further, a notion which exists already in the sound natural understanding, requiring rather to be cleared up than to be taught, and which in estimating the value of our actions always takes the first place, and constitutes the condition of all the rest. In order to do this we will take the notion of duty, which includes that of a good will, although implying certain subjective restrictions and hindrances. These, however, far from concealing it, or rendering it unrecognizable, rather bring it out by contrast, and make it shine forth so much the brighter.

I omit here all actions which are already recognized as inconsistent with duty, although they may be useful for this or that purpose, for with these the question whether they are done from duty cannot arise at all, since they even conflict with it. I also set aside those actions which really conform to duty, but to which men have no direct inclination, performing them because they are impelled thereto by some other inclination. for in this case we can readily distinguish

whether the action which agrees with duty is done from duty, or from
a selfish view. It is much harder to make this distinction when the
action accords with duty, and the subject has besides a direct
inclination to it. For example, it is always a matter of duty that a
dealer should not overcharge an inexperienced purchaser, and
wherever there is much commerce the prudent tradesman does not
overcharge, but keeps a fixed price for everyone, so that a child buys
of him as well as any other. Men are thus honestly served; but this is
not enough to make us believe that the tradesman has so acted from
duty and from principles of honesty: his own advantage required it; it
is out of the question in this case to suppose that he might besides
have a direct inclination in favor of the buyers, so that, as it were,
from love he should give no advantage to one over another.
Accordingly the action was done neither from duty nor from direct
inclination, but merely with a selfish view.

On the other hand, it is a duty to maintain one's life; and, in
addition, every one has also a direct inclination to do so. but on this
account the often anxious care which most men take for it has no
intrinsic worth, and their maxim has no moral import. They preserve
their life as duty requires, no doubt, but not because duty requires.
On the other hand, if adversity and hopeless sorrow have completely
taken away the relish for life, if the unfortunate one, strong in mind,
indignant at his fate rather than desponding or dejected, wishes for
death, and yet preserves his life without loving it—not from
inclination or fear, but from duty—then his maxim has a moral
worth.

To be beneficent when we can is a duty; and besides this, there
are many minds so sympathetically constituted that, without any
other motive of vanity or self-interest, they find a pleasure in
spreading joy around them, and can take delight in the satisfaction
of others so far as it is their own work. but I maintain that in such a
case an action of this kind, however proper, however amiable it may
be, has nevertheless no true moral worth, but is on a level with other
inclinations, e.g. the inclination to honor, which , if it is happily
directed to that which is in fact of public utility and accordant with
duty, and consequently honorable, deserves praise and
encouragement, but not esteem. for the maxim lacks the moral
import, namely, that such actions be done from duty, not from

inclination. Put the case that the mind of that philanthropist were clouded by sorrow of his own extinguishing all sympathy with the lot of others, and that while he still has the power to benefit others in
110   distress, he is not touched by their trouble because he is absorbed with his own; and now suppose that he tears himself out of this dead insensibility, and performs the action without any inclination to it, but simply from duty, then first has his action its genuine moral worth. Further still; if nature has put little sympathy in the heart of
115   this or that man; if he, supposed to be an upright man, is by temperament cold and indifferent to the sufferings of others, perhaps because in respect of his own he is provided with the special gift of patience and fortitude, and supposes, or even requires, that others should have the same—and such a man would certainly not be the
120   meanest product of nature—but if nature had not specially framed him for a philanthropist, would he not still find in himself a source fro whence to give himself a far higher worth than that of a good-natured temperament could be? Unquestionable. It is just in this that the moral worth of the character is brought out which is
125   incomparably the highest of all, namely, that he is beneficent, not from inclination, but from duty.

      To secure one's own happiness is a duty, at least indirectly; for discontent with one's condition, under a pressure of many anxieties and amidst unsatisfied wants, might easily become a great
130   temptation to transgression of duty. But here again, without looking to duty, all men have already the strongest and most intimate inclination to happiness, because it is just in this idea that all inclinations are combined in one total. But the precept of happiness is often of such a sort that it greatly interferes with some
135   inclinations, and yet a man cannot form any definite and certain conception of the sum of satisfaction of all of them which is called happiness. It is not then to be wondered at that a single inclination, definite both as to what it promises and as to the time within which it can be gratified, is often able to overcome such a fluctuating idea,
140   and that a gouty patient, for instance, can choose to enjoy what he likes, and to suffer what he may, since according to his calculation, on this occasion at least, he has (only) not sacrificed the enjoyment of the present moment to a possible mistaken expectation of a happiness which is supposed to be found in health. But even in this

145 case, if the general desire for happiness did not influence his will,
and supposing that in his particular case health was not a necessary
element in this calculation, there yet remains in this, as in all other
cases, this law, namely, that he should promote his happiness not
from inclination but from duty, and by this would his conduct first
150 acquire true moral worth.

It is in this manner, undoubtedly, that we are to understand
those passages of Scripture also in which we are commanded to love
our neighbor, even our enemy. For love, as an affection, cannot be
commanded, but beneficence for duty's sake may; even though we are
155 not impelled to it by any inclination—nay, are even repelled by a
natural and unconquerable aversion. This is practical love, and not
pathological—a love which is seated in the will, and not in the
propensions of sense—in principles of action and not of tender
sympathy; and it is this love alone which can be commanded.

160 The second proposition is, that an action done from duty derives
its moral worth, not from the purpose which is to be attained by it,
but from the maxim by which it is determined, and therefore does not
depend on the realization of the object of the action, but merely on
the principle of volition by which the action has taken place, without
165 regard to any object of desire. It is clear from what precedes that the
purposes which we may have in view in our actions, or their effects
regarded as ends and springs of the will, cannot give to actions any
unconditional or moral worth. In what, then, can their worth lie, if it
is not to consist in the will and in reference to its expected effect? It
170 cannot lie anywhere but in the principle of the will without regard to
the ends which can be attained by the action. For the will stands
between its a priori principle, which is formal, and its *a posteriori*
spring, which is material, as between two roads, and as it must be
determined by something, it follows that it must be determined by
175 something, it follows that it must be determined by the formal
principle of volition when an action is done from duty, in which case
every material principle has been withdrawn from it.

The third proposition, which is a consequence of the two
preceding, I would express thus: Duty is the necessity of acting from
180 respect for the law. I may have inclination for an object as the effect
of my proposed action, but I cannot have respect for it, just for this
reason, I cannot have respect for inclination, whether my own or

another's; I can at most, if my own, approve it; if another's, sometimes even love it; i.e. look on it as favorable to my own interest.
It is only what is connected with my will as a principle, by no means as an effect—what does not subserve my inclination, but overpowers it, or at least in case of choice excludes it from its calculation—in other words, simply the law of itself which can be an object of respect, and hence a command. Now an action done from duty must wholly exclude the influence of inclination, and with it every object of the will, so that nothing remains which can determine the will except objectively the law, and subjectively pure respect for this practical law, and consequently the maxim that I should follow this law even to the thwarting of all my inclinations.

Thus the moral worth of an action does not lie in the effect expected from it, nor in any principle of action which requires to borrow its motive from this expected effect. For all these effects—agreeableness of one's condition, and even the promotion of the happiness of others—could have been also brought about by other causes, so that for this there would have been no need of the will of a rational being; whereas it is in this alone that the supreme and unconditional good can be found. The pre-eminent good which we call moral can therefore consist in nothing else than the conception of law in itself, which certainly is only possible in a rational being, in so far as this conception, and not the expected effect, determines the will. This is a good which is already present in the person who acts accordingly, and we have not to wait for it to appear first in the result.

But what sort of law can that be, the conception of which must determine the will, even without paying any regard to the effect expected from it, in order that this will may be called good absolutely and without qualification? As I have deprived the will of every impulse which could arise to it from obedience to any law, there remains nothing but the universal conformity of its actions to law in general, which alone is to serve the will as a principle, i.e. I am never to act otherwise than so that I could also will that my maxim should become a universal law. Here now, it is the simple conformity to law in general, without assuming any law particular law applicable to certain actions, that serves the will as its principle, and must so serve it, if duty is not to be a vain delusion and a chimerical notion.

The common reason of men in its practical judgments perfectly coincides with this, and always has in view the principle here suggested. Let the question be, for example: May I when in distress make a promise with the intention not to keep it? I readily distinguish here between the two significations which the question may have: Whether it is prudent, or whether it is right, to make a false promise. The former may undoubtedly often be the case. I see clearly indeed that it is not enough to extricate myself from a present difficulty by means of this subterfuge, but it must be well considered whether there may not hereafter spring from this lie much greater inconvenience than that from which I now free myself, and as, with all my supposed cunning, the consequences cannot be so easily foreseen but that credit once lost may be much more injurious to me than any mischief which I seek to avoid at present, it should be considered whether it would not be more prudent to act herein according to a universal maxim, and to make it a habit to promise nothing except with the intention of keeping it. But it is soon clear to me that such a maxim will still only be based on the fear of consequences. Now it is a wholly different thing to be truthful from duty, and to be so from apprehension of injurious consequences. In the first case, the very notion of the action already implies a law for me; in the second case, I must first look about elsewhere to see what results may be combined with it which would affect myself. For to deviate from the principle of duty is beyond all doubt wicked; but to be unfaithful to my maxim of prudence may often be very advantageous to me, although to abide by it is certainly safer. The shortest way, however, and an unerring one, to discover the answer to this question whether a lying promise is consistent with duty, is to ask myself, should I be content that my maxim (to extricate myself from difficulty by a false promise) should hold good as a universal law, for myself as well as for others? and should I be able to myself, "Every one may make a deceitful promise when he finds himself in a difficulty from which he cannot otherwise extricate himself?" Then I presently become aware that while I can will the lie, I can by no means will that lying should be a universal law. For with such a law there would be no promises at all, since it would be in vain to allege my intention in regard to my future actions to those who would not believe this allegation, or if they over-hastily did so would pay me

back in my own coin. Hence my maxim, as soon as it should be made
a universal law, would necessarily destroy itself.

I do not, therefore, need any far-reaching penetration to discern
what I have to do in order that my will may be morally good.
Inexperienced in the course of the world, incapable of being prepared
for all its contingencies, I only ask myself: Can you also will that your
maxim should be a universal law? If not, then it must be rejected,
and that not because of a disadvantage accruing from it to myself or
even to others, but because it cannot enter as a principle into a
possible universal legislation, and reason extorts from me immediate
respect for such legislation. I do not indeed as yet discern on what
this respect is based (this the philosopher may inquire), but at least
I understand this, that it is an estimation of the worth which far
outweighs all worth of what is recommended by inclination, and that
the necessity of acting from pure respect for the practical law is what
constitutes duty, to which every other motive must give place,
because it is the condition of a will being good in itself, and the worth
of such a will is above everything.

John Stuart Mill, *Utilitarianism*

CHAPTER I—GENERAL REMARKS

There are few circumstances among those which make up the present condition of human knowledge, more unlike what might have been expected, or more significant of the backward state in which speculation on the most important subjects still lingers, than the
5   little progress which has been made in the decision of the controversy respecting the criterion of right and wrong. From the dawn of philosophy, the question concerning the *summum bonum*, or, what is the same thing, concerning the foundation of morality, has been accounted the main problem in speculative thought, has occupied the
10 most gifted intellects, and divided them into sects and schools, carrying on a vigorous warfare against one another. And after more than two thousand years the same discussions continue, philosophers are still ranged under the same contending banners, and neither thinkers nor mankind at large seem nearer to being
15 unanimous on the subject, than when the youth Socrates listened to the old Protagoras, and asserted (if Plato's dialogue be grounded on a real conversation) the theory of utilitarianism against the popular morality of the so-called sophist.

It is true that similar confusion and uncertainty, and in some
20 cases similar discordance, exist respecting the first principles of all the sciences, not excepting that which is deemed the most certain of them, mathematics; without much impairing, generally indeed without impairing at all, the trustworthiness of the conclusions of those sciences. An apparent anomaly, the explanation of which is
25 that the detailed doctrines of a science are not usually deduced from, nor depend for their evidence upon, what are called its first principles. Were it not so, there would be no science more precarious, or whose conclusions were more insufficiently made out, than algebra; which derives none of its certainty from what are commonly
30 taught to learners as its elements, since these, as laid down by some of its most eminent teachers, are as full of fictions as English law, and of mysteries as theology. The truths which are ultimately accepted as the first principles of a science, are really the last results of metaphysical analysis, practiced on the elementary notions with

35   which the science is conversant; and their relation to the science is
        not that of foundations to an edifice, but of roots to a tree, which may
        perform their office equally well though they be never dug down to
        and exposed to light. But though in science the particular truths
        precede the general theory, the contrary might be expected to be the
40   case with a practical art, such as morals or legislation. All action is
        for the sake of some end, and rules of action, it seems natural to
        suppose, must take their whole character and color from the end to
        which they are subservient. When we engage in a pursuit, a clear
        and precise conception of what we are pursuing would seem to be the
45   first thing we need, instead of the last we are to look forward to. A
        test of right and wrong must be the means, one would think, of
        ascertaining what is right or wrong, and not a consequence of having
        already ascertained it.
                The difficulty is not avoided by having recourse to the popular
50   theory of a natural faculty, a sense or instinct, informing us of right
        and wrong. For—besides that the existence of such a moral instinct
        is itself one of the matters in dispute—those believers in it who have
        any pretensions to philosophy, have been obliged to abandon the
        idea that it discerns what is right or wrong in the particular case in
55   hand, as our other senses discern the sight or sound actually present.
        Our moral faculty, according to all those of its interpreters who are
        entitled to the name of thinkers, supplies us only with the general
        principles of moral judgments; it is a branch of our reason, not of our
        sensitive faculty; and must be looked to for the abstract doctrines of
60   morality, not for perception of it in the concrete. The intuitive, no less
        than what may be termed the inductive, school of ethics, insists on
        the necessity of general laws. They both agree that the morality of an
        individual action is not a question of direct perception, but of the
        application of a law to an individual case. they recognize also, to a
65   great extent, the same moral laws; but differ as to their evidence,
        and the source from which they derive their authority. According to
        the one opinion, the principles of morals are evident a priori,
        requiring nothing to command assent, except that the meaning of the
        terms be understood. According to the other doctrine, right and
70   wrong, as well as truth and falsehood, are questions of observation
        and experience. but both hold equally that morality must be deduced
        from principles; and the intuitive school affirm as strongly as the

inductive that there is a science of morals. Yet they seldom attempt to make out a list of the a priori principles which are to serve as the premises of the science; still more rarely do they make any effort to reduce those various principles to one first principle, or common ground of obligation. They either assume the ordinary precepts of morals as of a priori authority, or they lay down as the common groundwork of those maxims some generality much less obviously authoritative than the maxims themselves, and which has never succeeded in gaining popular acceptance. Yet to support their pretensions there ought either to be some one fundamental principle or law, at the root of all morality, or if there be several, there should be a determinate order of precedence among them; and the one principal, or the rule for deciding between the various principles when they conflict, ought to be self-evident.

To acquire how far the bad effects of this deficiency have been mitigated in practice, or to what extent the moral beliefs of mankind have been vitiated or made uncertain by the absence of any distinct recognition of an ultimate standard, would imply a complete survey and criticism of past and present ethical doctrine. It would, however, be easy to show that whatever steadiness or consistency these moral beliefs have attained, has been mainly due to the tacit influence of a standard not recognized. Although the nonexistence of an acknowledged first principle has made ethics not so much a guide as a consecration of men's actual sentiments, still, as men's sentiments, both of favor and of aversion, are greatly influenced by what they suppose to be the effects of things upon their happiness, the principle of utility, or as Bentham latterly called it, the greatest happiness principle, has had a large share in forming the moral doctrines even of those who most scornfully reject its authority. Nor is there any school of thought which refuses to admit that the influence of actions on happiness is a most material and even predominant consideration in many of the details of morals, however unwilling to acknowledge it as the fundamental principle of morality, and the source of moral obligation. I might go much further, and say that to all those a priori moralists who deem it necessary to argue at all, utilitarian arguments are indispensable. It is not my present purpose to criticize these thinkers; but I cannot help referring, for illustration, to a systematic treatise by one of the most illustrious of them, the

Metaphysics of Ethics, by Kant. This remarkable man, whose system of thought will long remain one of the landmarks in the history of philosophical speculation, does, in the treatise in question, lay down a universal first principle as the origin and ground of moral
115   obligation; it is this:—"So act, that the rule on which you act would admit of being adopted as a law by all rational beings." But when he begins to deduce from this precept any of the actual duties of morality, he fails, almost grotesquely, to show that there would be any contradiction, any logical (not to say physical) impossibility, in
120   the adoption by all rational beings of the most outrageously immoral rules of conduct. All he shows is that the consequences of their universal adoption would be such as no one would choose to incur.

On the present occasion, I shall, without further discussion of the other theories, attempt to contribute something towards the
125   understanding and appreciation of the utilitarian or happiness theory, and towards such proof as it is susceptible of. It is evident that this cannot be proof in the ordinary and popular meaning of the term. Questions of ultimate ends are not amenable to direct proof. whatever can be proved to be good, must be so by being shown to be
130   a means to something admitted to be good without proof. The medical art is proved to be good by its conducing to health; but how is it possible to prove that health is good? The art of music is good, for the reason, among others, that it produces pleasure; but what proof is it possible to give that pleasure is good? If, then, it is
135   asserted that there is a comprehensive formula, including all things which are in themselves good, and that whatever else is good, is not so as an end, but as a mean, the formula may be accepted or rejected, but is not a subject of what is commonly understood by proof. We are not, however, to infer that its acceptance or rejection
140   must depend on blind impulse, or arbitrary choice. There is a large meaning of the word proof, in which this question is as amenable to it as any other of the disputed questions of philosophy. The subject is within the cognizance of the rational faculty; and neither does that faculty deal with it solely in the way of intuition. Considerations may
145   be presented capable of determining the intellect either to give or withhold its assent to the doctrine; and this is equivalent to proof.

We shall examine presently of what nature are these considerations; in what manner they apply to the case, and what

rational grounds, therefore, can be given for accepting or rejecting the
150 utilitarian formula. But it is a preliminary condition of rational
acceptance or rejection, that the formula should be correctly
understood. I believe that the very imperfect notion ordinarily formed
of its meaning is the chief obstacle which impedes its reception; and
that could it be cleared, even from only the grosser misconceptions,
155 the question would be greatly simplified, and a large proportion of its
difficulties removed. Before, therefore, I attempt to enter into the
philosophical grounds which can be given for assenting to the
utilitarian standard, I shall offer some illustrations of the doctrine
itself; with the view of showing more clearly what it is, distinguishing
160 it from what it is not, and disposing of such of the practical objections
to it as either originate in, or are closely connected with, mistaken
interpretations of its meaning. Having thus prepared the ground, I
shall afterwards endeavor to throw such light as I can upon the
question, considered as one of philosophical theory.

CHAPTER II—WHAT UTILITARIANISM IS

165 A passing remark is all that needs be given to the ignorant
blunder of supposing that those who stand up for utility as the test
of right and wrong, use the term in that restricted and merely
colloquial sense in which utility is opposed to pleasure. an apology is
due to the philosophical opponents of utilitarianism, for even the
170 momentary appearance of confounding them with anyone capable of
so absurd a misconception; which is the more extraordinary,
inasmuch as the contrary accusation, of referring everything to
pleasure, and that too in its grossest form, is another of the common
charges against utilitarianism: and, as has been pointedly remarked
175 by an able writer, the same sort of persons, and often the very same
persons, denounce the theory "as impracticably dry when the word
utility precedes the word pleasure, and as too practicably voluptuous
when the word pleasure precedes the word utility." Those who know
anything about the matter are aware that every writer, from
180 Epicurus to Bentham, who maintained the theory of utility, meant by
it, not something to be contradistinguished from pleasure, but
pleasure itself, together with exemption from pain; and instead of
opposing the useful to the agreeable or the ornamental, have always

declared that the useful means these, among other things. Yet the
common herd, including the herd of writers, not only in newspapers,
and periodicals, but in books of weight and pretension, are
perpetually falling into this shallow mistake. Having caught up the
word 'utilitarian', while knowing nothing whatever about it but its
sound, they habitually express by it the rejection, or the neglect, of
pleasure in some of its forms: of beauty, of ornament, or of
amusement. Nor is the term thus ignorantly misapplied solely in
disparagement, but occasionally in compliment; as though it implied
superiority to frivolity and the mere pleasures of the moment. And
this perverted use if the only one in which the word is popularly
known, and the one from which the new generation are acquiring
their sole notion of its meaning. Those who introduced the word, but
who had for many years discontinued it as a distinctive appellation,
may well feel themselves called upon to resume it, if by doing so they
can hope to contribute anything towards rescuing it from this utter
degradation.

The creed which accepts as the foundation of morals utility, or
the greatest happiness principle, holds that actions are right in
proportion as they tend to promote happiness, wrong as they tend to
produce the reverse of happiness. by 'happiness' is intended
pleasure, and the absence of pain; by 'unhappiness', pain, and the
privation of pleasure. To give a clear view of the moral standard set
up by the theory, much more requires to be said; in particular, what
things it includes in the ideas of pain and pleasure; and to what
extent this is left an open question. But these supplementary
explanations do not affect the theory of life on which this theory of
morality is grounded—namely, that pleasure, and freedom from pain,
are the only things desirable as ends; and that all desirable things
(which are as numerous in the utilitarian as in any other scheme) are
desirable either for the pleasure inherent in themselves, or as means
to the promotion of pleasure and the prevention of pain.

Now such a theory of life excites in many minds, and among them
in some of the most estimable in feeling and purpose, inveterate
dislike. To suppose that life has (as they express it) no higher end
than pleasure—no better and nobler object of desire and
pursuit—they designate as utterly mean and groveling; as a doctrine
worthy only of swine, to whom the followers of Epicurus were, at a

very early period, contemptuously likened; and modern holders of the doctrine are occasionally made the subject of equally polite comparisons by its German, French, and English assailants.

225   When thus attacked, the Epicureans have always answered that it is not they but their accusers who represent human nature in a degrading light; since the accusation supposes human beings to be capable of no pleasures except those of which swine are capable. If this supposition were true, the charge could not be gainsaid, but

230 would then be no longer an imputation; for if the sources of pleasure were precisely the same to human beings and to swine, the rule of life which is good enough for the one would be good enough for the other. The comparison of the Epicurean life to that of beasts is felt as degrading, precisely because a beast's pleasures do not satisfy a

235 human being's conceptions of happiness. Human beings have faculties more elevated than the animal appetites, and when once made conscious of them, do not regard anything as happiness which does not include their gratification. I do not, indeed, consider the Epicureans to have been by any means faultless in drawing out their

240 scheme of consequences from the utilitarian principle. To do this in any sufficient manner, many Stoic, as well as Christian elements require to be included. But there is no known Epicurean theory of life which does not assign to the pleasures of the intellect, of the feelings and imagination, and of the moral sentiments, a much higher value

245 as pleasures than to those of mere sensation. It must be admitted, however, that utilitarian writers in general have placed the superiority of mental over bodily pleasures chiefly in the greater permanency, safety, uncostliness, etc., of the former—that is, in their circumstantial advantages rather than in their intrinsic nature. And

250 on all these points utilitarians have fully proved their case; but they might have taken the other, and, as it may be called, higher ground, with entire consistency. It is quite compatible with the principle of utility to recognize the fact, that some kinds of pleasure are more desirable and more valuable than others. It would be absurd that

255 while, in estimating all other things, quality is considered as well as quantity, the estimation of pleasures should be supposed to depend on quantity alone.

    If I am asked what I mean by difference of quality in pleasures, or what makes one pleasure more valuable than another merely as a

260 pleasure, except its being greater in amount, there is but one possible answer. Of two pleasures, if there by one to which all or almost all who have experience of both give a decided preference, irrespective of any feeling of moral obligation to prefer it, that is the more desirable pleasure. If one of the two is, by those who are
265 competently acquainted with both, placed so far above the other that they prefer it, even though knowing it to be attended with a greater amount of discontent, and would not resign it for any quantity of the other pleasure which their nature is capable of, we are justified in ascribing to the preferred enjoyment a superiority in quality, so far
270 outweighing quantity as to render it, in comparison, of small account.

Now it is an unquestionable fact that those who are equally acquainted with, and equally capable of appreciating and enjoying, both, do give a most marked preference to the manner of existence which employs their higher faculties. Few human creatures would
275 consent to be changed into any of the lower animals, for a promise of the fullest allowance of a beast's pleasures; no intelligent human being would consent to be a fool, no instructed person would be an ignoramus, no person of feeling and conscience would be selfish and base, even though they should be persuaded that the fool, the dunce,
280 or the rascal is better satisfied with his lot than they are with theirs. They would not resign what they possess more than he for the most complete satisfaction of all the desires which they have in common with him. If they ever fancy they would, it is only in cases of unhappiness so extreme, that to escape from it they would exchange
285 their lot for almost any other, however undesirable in their own eyes. A being of higher faculties requires more to make him happy, is capable probably of more acute suffering, and certainly accessible to it at more points, than one of an inferior type; but in spite of these liabilities, he can never really wish to sink into what he feels to be a
290 lower grade of existence. We may give what explanation we please of this unwillingness: we may attribute it to pride, a name which is given indiscriminately to some of the most and to some of the least estimable feelings of which mankind are capable; we may refer it to the love of liberty and personal independence, an appeal to which
295 was with the Stoics one of the most effective means for the inculcation of it; to the love of power, or to the love of excitement, both of which do really enter into and contribute to it: but its most

appropriate appellation is a sense of dignity, which all human beings possess in one form or other, and in some, though by no means in
300   exact, proportion to their higher faculties, and which is so essential a part of the happiness of those in whom it is strong, that nothing which conflicts with it could be, otherwise than momentarily, an object of desire to them. Whoever supposes that this preference takes place at a sacrifice of happiness—that the superior being, in anything
305   like equal circumstances, is not happier than the inferior—confounds the two very different ideas, of happiness and content. It is indisputable that the being whose capacities of enjoyment are low, has the greatest chance of having them fully satisfied; and a highly endowed being will always feel that any happiness which he can look
310   for, as the world is constituted, is imperfect. but he can learn to bear its imperfections, if they are at all bearable; and they will not make him envy the being who is indeed unconscious of the imperfections, but only because he feels not at all the good which those imperfections qualify. It is better to be a human being dissatisfied
315   than a pig satisfied; better to be Socrates dissatisfied than a fool satisfied. And if the fool, or the pig, are of a different opinion, it is because they only know their own side of the question. The other party to the comparison knows both sides.

        It may be objected that many who are capable of the higher
320   pleasures, occasionally, under the influence of temptation, postpone them to the lower. But his is quite compatible with a full appreciation of the intrinsic superiority of the higher. Men often, from infirmity of character, make their election for the nearer good, though they know it to be the less valuable; and this no less when the choice
325   is between two bodily pleasures, than when it is between bodily and mental. They pursue sensual indulgences to the injury of health, though perfectly aware that health is the greater good. It may be further objected that many who begin with youthful enthusiasm for everything noble, as they advance in years sink into indolence and
330   selfishness. But I do not believe that those who undergo this very common change, voluntarily choose the lower description of pleasures in preference to the higher. I believe that before they devote themselves exclusively to the one, they have already become incapable of the other. Capacity for the nobler feelings is in most
335   natures a very tender plant, easily killed, not only by hostile

influences. But by mere want of sustenance; and in the majority of young persons it speedily dies away if the occupations to which their position in life has devoted them, and the society into which it has thrown them, are not favorable to keeping that higher capacity in
340 exercise. Men lose their high aspirations as they lose their intellectual tastes, because they have not time or opportunity for indulging them; and they addict themselves to inferior pleasures not because they deliberately prefer them, but because they are either the only ones to which they have access or the only ones which they
345 are any longer capable of enjoying. It may be questioned whether anyone who has remained equally susceptible to both classes of pleasures, ever knowingly and calmly preferred the lower; though many, in all ages, have broken down in an ineffectual attempt to combine both.

350   From this verdict of the only competent judges I apprehend there can be no appeal. On a question which is the best worth having of two pleasures, or which of two modes of existence is the most grateful to the feelings, apart from its moral attributes and from its consequences, the judgment of those who are qualified by knowledge
355 of both, or, if they differ, that of the majority among them, must be admitted as final. And there need be the less hesitation to accept this judgment respecting the quality of pleasures, since there is no other tribunal to be referred to even on the question of quantity. What means are there of determining which is the acutest of two
360 pains, or the intensest of two pleasurable sensations, except the general suffrage of those who are familiar with both? Neither pains nor pleasures are homogenous, and pain is always heterogeneous with pleasure. What is there to decide whether a particular pleasure is worth purchasing at the cost of a particular pain, except the feeling
365 and judgment of the experienced? When, therefore, those feelings and judgment declare the pleasures derived from the higher faculties to be preferable in kind, apart from the question of intensity, to those of which the animal nature, disjoined from the higher faculties, is susceptible, they are entitled on this subject to the same regard.

370   I have dwelt on this point, as being a necessary part of a perfectly just conception of utility, or happiness, considered as the directive rule of human conduct. But it is by no means an indispensable condition to the acceptance of the utilitarian standard;

for that standard is not the agent's own greatest happiness, but the greatest amount of happiness altogether; and if it may possible be doubted whether a noble character is always the happier for its nobleness, there can be no doubt that it makes other people happier, and that the world in general is immensely a gainer by it. Utilitarianism, therefore, could only attain its end by the general cultivation of nobleness of character, even if each individual were only benefited by the nobleness of others, and his own, so far as happiness is concerned, were a sheer deduction from the benefit. But the bare enunciation of such an absurdity as this last renders refutation superfluous.

According to the 'greatest happiness principle', as above explained, the ultimate end, with reference to and for the sake of which all other things are desirable (whether we are considering our own good or that of other people), is an existence exempt as far as possible from pain, and as rich as possible in enjoyments, both in point of quantity and quality; the test of quality, and the rule for measuring it against quantity, being the preference felt by those who in their opportunities of experience, to which must be added their habits of self-consciousness and self-observation, are best furnished with the means of comparison. This, being, according to the utilitarian opinion, the end of human action, is necessarily also the standard of morality; which may accordingly be defined, the rules and precepts for human conduct, by the observance of which an existence such as has been described might be, to the greatest extent possible, secured to all mankind; and not to them only, but, so far as the nature of things admits, to the whole sentient creation. ...

The objectors to utilitarianism cannot always be charged with representing it in a discreditable light. On the contrary, those among them who entertain anything like a just idea of its disinterested character sometimes find fault with its standard as being too high for humanity. They say it is exacting too much to require that people shall always act from the inducement of promoting the general interests of society. But this is to mistake the very meaning of a standard of morals, and confound the rule of action with the motive of it. It is the business of ethics to tell us what are our duties, or by what test we may know them; but no system of ethics requires that the sole motive of all we do shall be a feeling of duty; on the contrary,

ninety-nine hundredths of all our actions are done from other
motives, and rightly so done, if the rule of duty does not condemn
them. It is the more unjust to utilitarianism that this particular
415   misapprehension should be made a ground of objection to it,
inasmuch as utilitarian moralists have gone beyond almost all others
in affirming that the motive has nothing to do with the morality of
the action, though much with the worth of the agent. He who saves a
fellow creature from drowning does what is morally right, whether his
420   motive be duty, or the hope of being paid for his trouble; he who
betrays the friend that trusts him, is guilty of a crime, even if his
object be to serve another friend to whom he is under greater
obligations. but to speak only of actions done from the motive of duty,
and in direct obedience to principle: it is a misapprehension of the
425   utilitarian mode of thought, to conceive it as implying that people
should fix their minds upon so wide a generality as the world, or
society at large. The great majority of good actions are intended not
for the benefit of the world, but for that of individuals, of which the
good of the world is made up; and the thoughts of the most virtuous
430   man need not on these occasions travel beyond the particular persons
concerned, except so far as is necessary to assure himself that in
benefiting them he is not violating the rights, that is, the legitimate
and authorized expectations, of anyone else. The multiplication of
happiness is, according to the utilitarian ethics, the object of virtue:
435   the occasions on which any person (except one in a thousand) has it
in his power to do this on an extended scale, in other words to be a
public benefactor, are but exceptional, and on these occasions alone
is he called on to consider public utility; in every other case, private
utility, the interest or happiness of some few persons, is all he has to
440   attend to. Those alone the influence of whose actions extends to
society in general, need concern themselves habitually about so large
an object. In the case of abstinences indeed—of things which people
forbear to do from moral considerations, though the consequences in
the particular case might be beneficial—it would be unworthy of an
445   intelligent agent not to be consciously aware that the action is of a
class which, if practiced generally, would be generally injurious, and
that this is the ground of the obligation to abstain it. The amount of
regard for the public interest implied in this recognition is no greater

than is demanded by every system of morals, for they all enjoin to
450   abstain from whatever is manifestly pernicious to society.